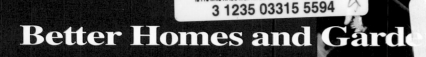

**Better Homes and Garden**

# PUTTIN' ON THE PAINT

## 101 PROJECTS & IDEAS for PAINTING on any surface

Meredith₀ Books
Des Moines, Iowa

# PUTTIN' ON THE PAINT

Editor: Carol Field Dahlstrom
Writer: Susan M. Banker
Designer: Angie Haupert Hoogensen
Copy Chief: Terri Fredrickson
Copy and Production Editor: Victoria Forlini
Editorial Operations Manager: Karen Schirm
Managers, Book Production: Pam Kvitne, Marjorie J. Schenkelberg, Rick von Holdt
Contributing Copy Editor: Arianna McKinney
Contributing Proofreaders: Beth Havey, Colleen Johnson, Anne Terpstra
Photographers: Andy Lyons Cameraworks, Scott Little
Technical Illustrator: Chris Neubauer Graphics, Inc.
Editorial and Design Assistants: Kaye Chabot, Mary Lee Gavin, Karen McFadden
Technical Assistant: Judy Bailey

## Meredith® Books
Editor in Chief: Linda Raglan Cunningham
Design Director: Matt Strelecki
Executive Editor, Food and Crafts: Jennifer Dorland Darling

Publisher: James D. Blume
Executive Director, Marketing: Jeffrey Myers
Executive Director, New Business Development: Todd M. Davis
Executive Director, Sales: Ken Zagor
Director, Operations: George A. Susral
Director, Production: Douglas M. Johnston
Business Director: Jim Leonard

Vice President and General Manager: Douglas J. Guendel

## Better Homes and Gardens® Magazine
Editor in Chief: Karol DeWulf Nickell

## Meredith Publishing Group
President, Publishing Group: Stephen M. Lacy
Vice President-Publishing Director: Bob Mate

## Meredith Corporation
Chairman and Chief Executive Officer: William T. Kerr

In Memoriam: E. T. Meredith III (1933-2003)

Library of Congress Control Number: 2003108769
ISBN: 0-696-21657-4

All of us at Better Homes and Gardens® Books are dedicated to providing you with information and ideas to create beautiful and useful projects. We welcome your comments and suggestions. Write to us at: Better Homes and Gardens Books, Crafts Editorial Department, 1716 Locust Street—LN112, Des Moines, IA 50309-3023.

If you would like to purchase any of our crafts, cooking, gardening, home improvement, or home decorating and design books, check wherever quality books are sold. Or visit us at: bhgbooks.com

Cover Photographs:
Andy Lyons Cameraworks
Scott Little

# GET READY TO PUT ON THE PAINT!

**W**e sponged, rolled, brushed, and sprayed. We masked, stenciled, layered, and dotted. We mixed colors, matched colors, and created colors. We've never had more fun *Puttin' on the Paint.* And we painted just about everything we could find! Look for cleverly painted walls, rugs, lamps, and chairs. Check out the colorful gourds, tables, and outdoor playhouses. We even painted a tire, a suitcase, and a couch!

In this book of painting projects and ideas, we'll show you how to spray-paint colorful planters that take only minutes but look like a million. Your plain picnic table can be a painted masterpiece with just a little paint and a few brushstrokes. And those ho-hum walls will be the talk of the neighborhood when you follow a few simple steps.

So grab your paint and your favorite painting tools and join us for some real painting fun as you start *Puttin' on the Paint!*

*Carol Field Dahlstrom*

# contents

5

# PAINT 101
## GETTING STARTED

If you love to paint or yearn to start, this chapter provides some insight into the fabulous world of paints and supplies. Hundreds of choices present themselves. This can be both wonderful and overwhelming without some background information to help you make choices. The following pages introduce you to the paints used in this book and will help you get your paintbrush into action.

# PaINT
## ProDUCTS

## PaINT ProDUCTS in SPraY form

Many kinds of spray paints and related products are available at art, crafts, automotive, and hardware stores. **a)** Stone-fleck paint comes in different colors to simulate a granite look. It leaves a rough texture. They can be found in art, crafts, and hardware stores.

**b)** Metalcast spray paint comes in red, yellow, and blue. It is a transparent brilliant-colored spray made to go over a chrome or silver base. It is found in automotive supply stores. **c)** Automotive spray paints are found in matte colors and metallics and are available in auto supply stores. **d)** Spray primer is a necessity for most projects. When used on slick surfaces, it creates a layer that bonds easily with most paints. It also evens out the base color, enabling better coverage and requiring less paint. Find it wherever paint is sold.
**e)** Lamé finish is a transparent paint with glitter flecks. Each sprayed coat adds more glitter to the surface. Buy it at crafts stores. **f)** Plastic paints are designed to adhere to plastic and are found in crafts and hardware stores. **g)** Glass paints work well on any slick surface, including glass. They come in various colors and are available with a glossy or frosted finish. They can be found in most crafts stores. **h)** Ultraviolet clear sealer is a good final coat to use on items prone to fading. However, it is not waterproof. It can be used on paper art and is found mostly in craft and fine art stores. **i)** Clear gloss coat is a glossy, heavy protective varnish and is available wherever paints are sold. **j)** Suede finish comes in a few earth tones and resembles suede. It can be purchased in crafts and paint stores. **k)** Bright metallic and other unusual colors are found in hobby sections where model cars are sold.
**l)** Spray paints are available in a wide selection of colors and finishes and adhere to many surfaces, including delicate silk flowers and fabrics. Art and crafts stores usually carry them. **m)** Pearlescent sprays work well on most surfaces; they have a pearl-like finish in several colors and are available in crafts stores. **n)** All-purpose spray paints are found in a limited range of colors. Pick these up in hardware stores. **o)** Chalkboard paint is a black paint meant to spray onto smooth surfaces, transforming them into a chalkboard. It is found in paint, hardware, and crafts stores. **p)** Metallic paints are found in different sheens and shades of gold, silver, bronze, copper, and pewter. These are available in crafts stores.

# paintproducts

## acrylic paints

Acrylics are inexpensive water-based paints that can be purchased in crafts and art stores. They dry quickly, and brushes can be cleaned in water. These paints are available in art and crafts stores.

## glossy fluorescent acrylic paints

Available in art and crafts stores, glossy fluorescent acrylic paints are quite durable and work well for outdoor projects.

## translucent paints

These are brilliant paints that work best on porous surfaces where they are easily absorbed. They do not evaporate, provide translucent color, and blend well. They do take time to dry. Look for these paints in art and stamping supply stores.

## transparent alcohol-based paint

A thin liquid, transparent alcohol-based paint can be used on many surfaces including glass. The paint dries rapidly, making it a challenging medium for some projects. Look for these in fine art or stamping supply stores.

## cream stencil oil-base paints

Cream stencil oil-base paints come in single pots or sets of small cakes. Use them with a stiff stencil brush on wood, walls, fabric, or other porous surfaces. These paints are available in crafts, fabric, and home improvement stores.

## water-soluble sun-sensitive paints

Water-soluble sun-sensitive paint are made to be used on fabric or paper. They work well with stencils and sunshine to leave pale relief shapes on a painted background. These paints are available in art and crafts stores.

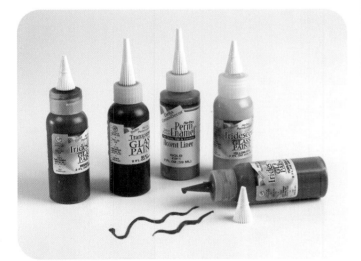

## glass paints

Glass paints in tubes are excellent for creating fine details on glass and slick surfaces. These paints are available in art and crafts stores.

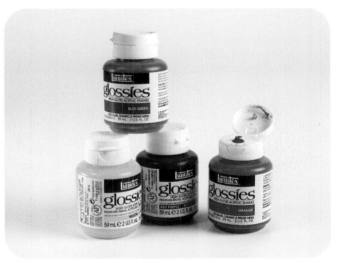

## acrylic enamel paints

Brilliant, glossy, and durable, acrylic enamels are appropriate for glass painting but require that the painted item be baked before use. These paints are available in art and crafts stores.

# paintproducts

## jar fabric paints

Jar fabric paints and dyes can be diluted with water for softer color or used straight for more intense results. The dyes dry soft to the touch. Pearlized colors have a slight texture. These paints are available in art and crafts stores.

## tube fabric paints

Fabric paint that comes in tubes has the consistency of thin pudding. Varieties include solid, glitter, pearl, glossy, and matte finishes. Fabric paints can be brushed on or used straight from the tube to create lines. These paints are available in art and crafts stores.

## glazes

Glazes offer numerous choices: Pearl or metallic; pastel or deep; large or small; pre-mixed or clear. Purchase clear glaze to use as is or mix it with paint for different tints and effects. These paints are available in art, crafts, and home improvement stores.

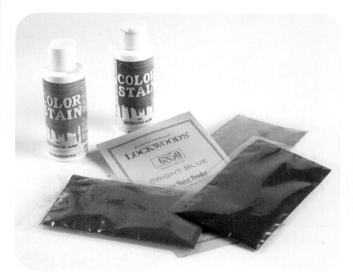

## color stains

Color stains come in almost any color. Some are bottled. Some come in packages to mix with water. They are found in crafts or woodworking supply stores.

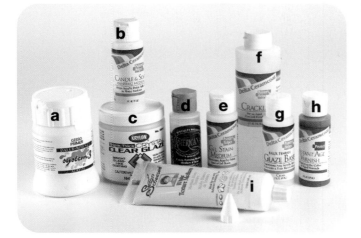

## surface enhancers

**a) Gesso primer** is a thick white primer made for canvas but it can coat most any surface.
**b) Candle painting medium** is mixed with acrylic paints to bond to waxy surfaces. **c) Clear glaze** is a glossy, thick varnish sealer. **d) Fabric painting medium** mixes with acrylic paint to make a more supple paint for fabric. **e) Gel stain medium** mixes with paint to create a translucent stain. **f) Crackle medium** painted onto a surface works as a base to create a crackle texture. **g) Glaze base** mixes with acrylic paint to make any color. **h) Antique varnish** gives an aged look. **i) Texture medium** is a white toothpaste-like medium for creating texture. It comes with different tips similar to frosting tips. These mediums are available in art and crafts stores.

## magnetic paint

Magnetic paint is made of metal particles, enabling magnets to stick to it. It is thick, heavy, and dark gray. This paint works on most sturdy surfaces. Paint over it with acrylics for color. These paints are available in art, crafts, and home improvement stores.

## permanent paint pens

Permanent paint pens work well on most surfaces. These are handy for decorating with smooth, bold lines. These pens are available in art and crafts stores.

## oil-base stick paints

Oil-base paint in stick form works like a crayon but dries more slowly. Because they have an oil base, they blend well. These sticks are available in art, crafts, and stamping supply stores.

# paintproducts

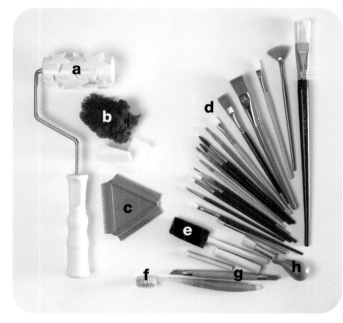

## specialty paint tools

Specialty paintbrushes and paint application tools come in many sizes, shapes, and materials. They are available in crafts and art stores. **a)** Sponge painting roller sleeves come in a variety of motifs, including stars. **b)** Natural sponges, available in crafts stores, create a pleasing effect on any surface. **c)** A rubber combing or graining tool drags across paint to reveal the base color in a grainlike pattern. **d)** Artist's brushes come in a variety of sizes and shapes, including round, flat, and fan. **e)** Foam brushes and dotters are inexpensive and disposable. The flat brushes are convenient to use when the paint finish is not important. The dotters stamp round spots. **f)** Toothbrushes are used for splattering paint. **g)** Rubber brushes are used to push paint, removing it from the surface. **h)** Stencil brushes have firm fibers to dab through stencil openings.

## wall paint tools

Often used on walls, the supplies above can be found in most paint departments. The rubber stamps (g and h) can also be purchased in crafts stores. House-painting brushes come in a variety of styles, sizes, and degrees of quality. Some have straight bristles and others are slanted. Experiment to learn which brushes work best with certain paint applications. **a)** A color-washing brush is used to blend colors in large areas. **b)** A good quality paintbrush with a keeper is a staple. Always store a cleaned brush in its cardboard keeper to insure it stays in good condition. **c)** A soft badger brush is for blending. **d)** A low-quality brush is used for special blending techniques and where the finish is not important. **e)** A chalk line reel makes straight lines on walls. **f)** Easy-release painter's tape protects areas where paint is not desired. **g–h)** Rubber stamps create designs with paint.

## Paint Rollers

Use thick roller sleeves for porous, rough surfaces, and medium-nap roller sleeves for smooth or finely textured walls. Double-headed rollers come with a double-welled paint pan for two-tone wall techniques. Rag roller sleeves give texture. To extend a roller for high walls, screw an extension rod into the handle. These products are available in paint supply stores.

## Paint Spray Gun

A paint spray gun can be purchased for as little as $40 in a paint supply store, holds about one quart of paint, and is powered by an air compressor. It is great for large surfaces or multiple projects. Wear a mask when spraying paint.

## Brush Spinner

This tool helps keep expensive brushes and roller sleeves in good condition. It is found in home improvement centers for a relatively small cost. This provides a quick, thorough way of cleaning and drying brushes and roller sleeves. Wash the brush or roller sleeve by hand to remove as much paint as possible. Insert the item into the slot on end or place sleeve over end, plunge into bucket of water, soak, and pump the handle back and forth, to spin the paint and water out of brush or roller. Repeat until clean and almost dry.

## Household Solvent

This product removes sticky substances, such as label glue and spots of dry paint,

but does not strip the surface. It also cleans dry paint from paintbrushes. The solvent is available in home improvement centers.

# MIX IT UP
## painting accessories
### for your home

No matter what your decorating style—vibrant color trends, traditional accents, or softer, subtle touches—you'll find a project to enhance your surroundings in this creative chapter. Discover how to coat candleholders with color and personalize the candlesticks they display. Learn how to transform an ordinary clear glass vase into a brilliant work of art that resembles stained glass. This chapter teaches you simple painting techniques that you can use to embellish picture frames, lamps, planters, and storage tables. Whether your project is new stools for the kids play area or a vibrant vase to display your roses, enjoy the skills you'll develop as you paint your way through these projects!

# COLOR BLOCK vase

## WHAT YOU'LL NEED

Clear glass vase

Masking tape; newspapers

Green glass spray paint, such as Krylon Stained Glass

Gold paint pen

Gold glass accent liner paint in bottle, such as Delta PermEnamel Accent Liner

## HERE'S HOW

1 Wash the vase and let it dry. Avoid touching the areas to be painted. Tape off the areas of the vase that you wish to remain clear.

2 In a well-ventilated work area, cover the work surface with newspapers. Spray the vase with green glass paint as shown in Photo A. Let dry. Spray on more coats until adequately covered, allowing to dry between coats; let dry. Remove the tape.

3 Use a gold paint pen to draw vertical lines where the glass is unpainted and to draw stems randomly on the green background. Use a bottle of accent liner paint to accentuate the edge of the green paint (Photo B) and to make groupings of three dots at the top of each stem. Let the paint dry 24 hours before using the vase.

PAINT A VASE WITH A GRAND
GEOMETRIC SHAPE AND EMBELLISH
IT WITH GOLDEN DETAILS.

# Fancy FLOOR Lamp

## WHAT YOU'LL NEED

Newspapers

Floor lamp with shade

Masking tape

Sheer spray paint, such as lamé, in pink glitter or other desired color

Acrylic paints in turquoise, ocher, peach, or other desired colors

Paintbrush

Gold highlighting medium, such as Rub 'n Buff

Sponge

Scissors

Pencil with round eraser

Broad tip gold felt paint pen

[continued on page 20]

COORDINATE A LAMP FOR ANY
DECORATING SCHEME BY ACCENTING
IT WITH SIMPLE SPONGE DESIGNS IN
YOUR FAVORITE COLORS.

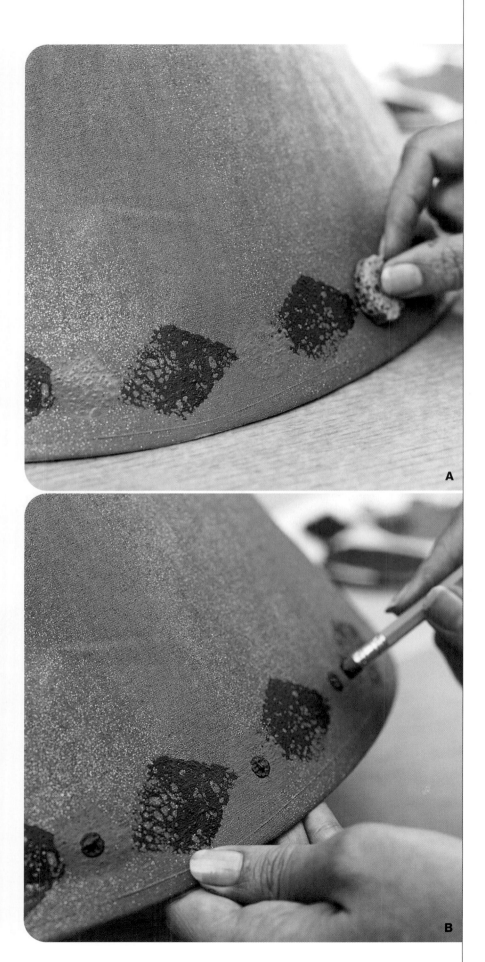

A

B

## Here's How

**1** In a well-ventilated work area, cover work surface with newspapers. Remove the shade from the lamp base and mask off the areas on the base that you want unpainted. Spray as many coats of sheer paint on the base as you wish, allowing to dry between coats. (This originally gold-tone lamp base was sprayed with only a couple of light coats of the sheer spray paint, giving it a transparent look.)

**2** Remove the masking tape and paint lamp base sections with turquoise and ocher acrylic paints.

**3** Paint the shade ocher. Let the paint dry. Paint additional coats if needed to obtain an even color, allowing the paint to dry between coats.

**4** Rub a small amount of gold highlighting medium on the raised areas of the lamp base. Let dry.

**5** Cut out small diamond and circle shapes from a kitchen sponge. Dab the shapes into acrylic paints and press onto the bottom edge of the shade to create a border pattern, alternating the circle and diamond as shown in Photo A, *opposite*. To make the turquoise dot, dip a pencil eraser into paint and dot onto shade as shown in Photo B. Let dry.

6 If directed by the paint manufacturer, shake the paint pen. Outline the shapes with gold as shown in Photo C. Let the outlines dry.

7 Spray the shade with the same sheer paint used on the lamp base. Holding the paint can 10 inches from the lamp shade, spray on light even coats, allowing the paint to dry between coats. Spray until the desired look is achieved. Let the paint dry.

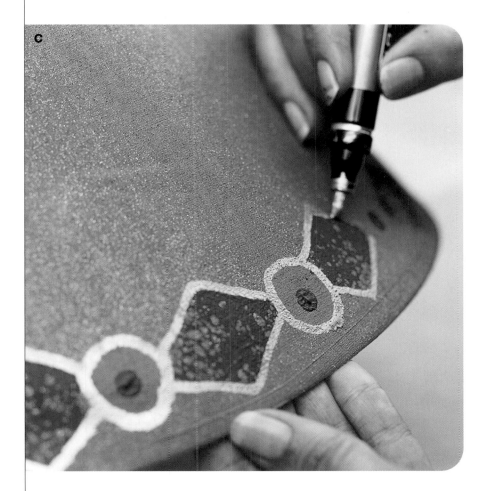

c

FOR OTHER SHADE DESIGNS, CARRY OUT A PATTERN FOUND IN YOUR ROOM, SUCH AS ONE ON A THROW PILLOW OR RUG.

# HIGHLIGHTED Hues Frame

## Here's HOW

**1** Paint the textured frame deep purple. Let the paint dry.

**2** Using a small amount of teal paint on brush, paint over purple base color highlighting raised areas as shown in Photo A. Let the paint dry.

**3** Coat entire frame with plum glaze. When glaze begins to dry, wipe off excess with a damp rag, allowing glaze to remain in crevices as shown in Photo B. Let dry.

**4** If desired, put on a latex glove. Using your finger, rub the raised areas of the frame with copper highlighting medium as shown in Photo C. Let dry.

## WHAT YOU'LL need

Textured frame

Acrylic paints in deep purple and teal

Paintbrush

Plum-color glaze

Rag

Latex glove, optional

Copper highlighting medium, such as Rub 'n Buff

PAINT, GLAZE, AND HIGHLIGHT A
TEXTURED PICTURE FRAME TO BRING OUT
DETAILS AND MAKE THEM SPARKLE.

# DOODLE-DE-DO TOY BOX

## WHAT YOU'LL need

Decorative storage table; paint stripper, if needed

Medium grit sandpaper

Tack cloth; paintbrushes

Water-based primer

Latex wall paint in desired colors

Masking tape; short nap roller

Black chalkboard paint, available in paint stores

Wood letters to spell "toy box"

Black acrylic paint; pencil; wood glue

## Here's HOW

1 If necessary, strip the surface of the storage table according to the product manufacturer's directions. Sand the surface of the table until it is smooth. Wipe away dust with a tack cloth.

2 Paint a coat of primer on the wood surfaces. Let the primer dry. Paint the sections with different colors of wall paint as desired; let dry.

3 Mask around areas where chalkboard paint is desired. Roll chalkboard paint onto each surface in even strokes, overlapping as little as possible as shown in Photo A. Let dry. Apply a second coat.

4 Sand and prime the wood letters; let dry. Paint the letters black; let dry. Dip a pencil eraser into wall paint and dot on letters; let dry. Glue on the letters; let dry.

USE AN OUTDATED OR PURCHASED
STORAGE TABLE FOR A PLAYFUL PLACE
TO KEEP TOYS OUT OF SIGHT.

# geranium
## Tin

## WHAT YOU'LL NEED

Newspapers

Metal container

White spray primer, such as KILZ

Large silk flowers

Scissors; gesso

Paintbrushes

Decorative trim, such as suede eyelet lace

Acrylic paints in cream, red, and green

Gold-tone glaze

Coarse, wide stiff paintbrush

Brown antiquing gel; rag

## HERE'S HOW

1 In a well-ventilated work area, cover the work surface with newspapers. Spray the container with two light coats of primer, allowing to dry between coats.

[continued on page 28]

PLANT SOME COLORFUL BLOOMS IN
A PLANTER THAT IS OVERLAID WITH
A BEAUTIFUL PATINA.

2 Remove three flower heads from stems, separating the layers. Coat both sides of the silk with gesso as shown in Photo A. Let dry.

3 Paint a thick coat of gesso on the container where flowers are desired. Place flowers and leaves on the tin and paint gesso over them. Let dry.

4 Cut trim to fit around the edge of the container. Paint gesso on container edge, wrap with trim, and paint over it with gesso as shown in Photo B. Paint random strokes of gesso onto the smooth areas of the container to create texture. Let dry.

USE THIS SAME TECHNIQUE TO MAKE A FLAT WORK OF ART TO FRAME AND HANG ON THE WALL.

5 Paint the entire container with cream acrylic paint as shown in Photo C, *opposite*. Let dry. Paint the flowers and trim red and the leaves green. Let dry.

6 Use a coarse, stiff flat paintbrush with a little gold-tone glaze on it and brush randomly over flowers and container as shown in Photo D. Let dry.

7 Paint over the container one section at a time with brown antiquing gel as shown in Photo E.

8 Before the gel completely dries, use a damp rag to wipe off the excess gel as shown in Photo F.

# nursery rhyme stools

## what you'll need

Newspapers

Stools

Spray primer, such as KILZ

Acrylic paints in pale aqua and pale green, peach and yellow, and mauve and lavender

Sponge; disposable plate

Wide paintbrush

Photocopies of patterns provided (photocopies must be from a toner-based copier, rather than ink jet)

Masking tape; scissors

Paint remover, such as Goof Off

Cotton swabs and paper towel

Pencil; card stock; crafts knife; tape

Stencil creams in peach, blue, green and white; small stencil brush; paper

Pearl white spray paint

Gloss glaze coat, such as Folk Art Clearcoate Hi-Shine Glaze spray

[continued on page 32]

CREATE THREE PLAYFUL STOOLS ADORNED
WITH THE NURSERY-RHYME CHARACTERS
WINKIN, BLINKIN, AND NOD.

**1** In a well-ventilated work area, cover surface with newspapers. For each stool, remove rubber feet if necessary. Spray entire stool with two light coats of primer, allowing to dry between coats.

**2** For each stool seat, use the pairs of colors listed on *page 30* or choose your own combinations. Spread about two tablespoons of each paint color onto a plate. To sponge-paint the seat, dab the sponge in one color of paint and then onto stool surface in a random pattern. Before paint dries, sponge on the other color, overlapping and blending the two colors as shown in Photo A. Use the wide paintbrush to paint stripes on each stool edge as shown in Photo B. Let the paint dry at least 48 hours to enable the paint to harden before transferring the face design.

**3** At a photocopy shop, get a toner-based copy of the desired face pattern from *pages 33, 35,* and *37* (an ink-based copy will bleed). Print extra copies and test the transfer method (see *page 34*) on another painted surface until comfortable with the

[continued on page 34]

winkin patterns

method and achieving good results. Trim the copy if needed; tape it to the stool seat, design side down.

4 To transfer the design, dip the cotton swab in paint remover and rub the cotton swab only over the printed areas of the design as shown in Photo C. Work quickly and firmly to avoid having paint remover soak into or sit wet on paint. The cotton swab should act like a marking pen, making a wet mark but drying quickly. Keep the swab moving rather than allowing it to rest on the paper. Check the transfer by lifting one edge of the paper while keeping it taped in position. Continue rubbing over all printed areas until all toner is transferred. Remove paper. Touch up faint areas with a sharp lead pencil, if desired.

5 Photocopy the words and stars onto card stock. To make a stencil, cut out the letters with a crafts knife, cutting away the black outline so it does not bleed into the stencil cream.

6 Tape the word and star stencils onto the stool surface. Use stencil cream in desired color to fill in the word. Dab small stencil brush into stencil

[continued on page 36]

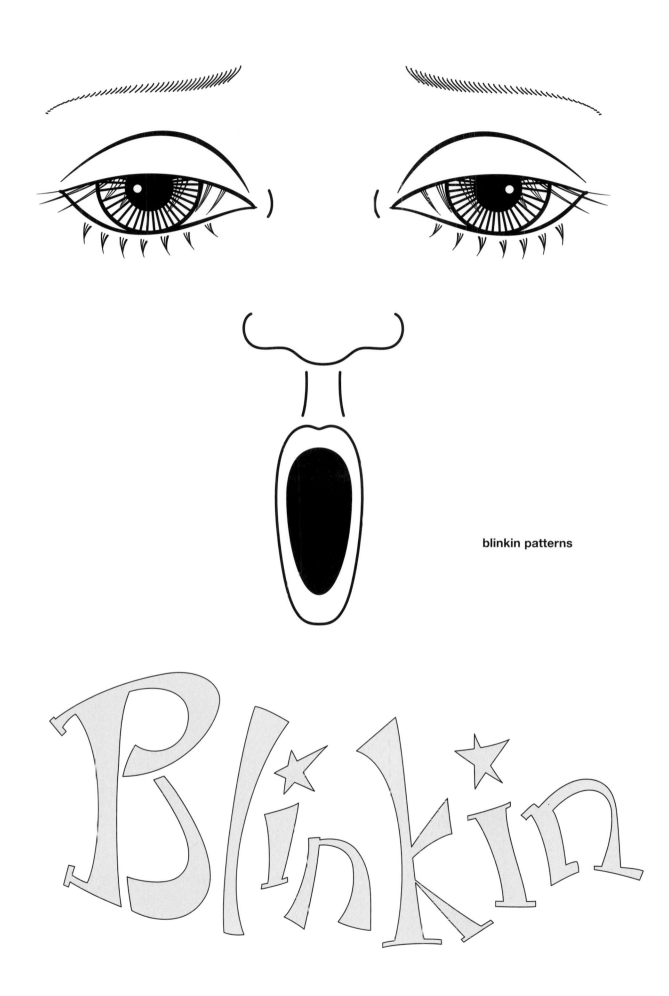

blinkin patterns

D

E

cream and stencil in color, brushing from outside inward to center of letter.

7 To create contour to faces, use the darker color to subtly apply shading under eyebrows, nose, and chin as shown in Photo D. Highlight eyelids, cheeks, nose, and chin with white. Use a very small amount at a time to achieve a soft, blended look. Keep applying layers of color until the desired look is achieved. Stencil stars as shown in Photo E. Let dry.

8 Cover the seat portion of stool with paper and tape. Spray two to three light coats of pearl white spray paint on the stool legs, allowing to dry between coats. Remove tape and paper.

9 To varnish, hold the can about 10 inches away and spray the stool with a light coat of varnish; let dry. Note: It is important to spray lightly or the face image may bleed. Repeat twice. Let dry. Place rubber feet back on stool legs.

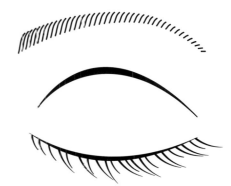
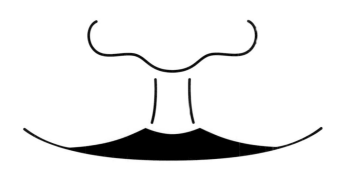

nod patterns

star patterns

# aT-THe-BeaCH BeaUTY

## WHaT YOU'LL need

Large frame with wide flat surfaces

Newspapers

White spray primer, such as KILZ

Sponge; water

Acrylic paints in pink, pale yellow, ivory, and pale blue

Narrow paintbrush

Seashells and pearl beads

Strong adhesive, such as E6000

## Here's HOW

**1** Remove the glass from the frame. In a well-ventilated work area, cover the work surface with newspapers. Allowing the primer to dry between coats, spray the frame with light even coats until it appears solid white.

**2** Soak sponge in water and squeeze out excess. Dab sponge in a color and sponge onto surface as shown in Photo A, blending in the desired order. Rinse out the sponge occasionally to keep the colors clean. Sponge paint continually, keeping paint wet and blending until a soft effect is achieved as shown in Photo B. Let the paint dry.

**3** Use a narrow paintbrush to paint random wavy ivory lines as shown in Photo C. If the frame has an inner border, paint it ivory. Let paint dry.

**4** Glue small shells and pearls in corners. Let the adhesive dry.

SPONGE-PAINT A PHOTO FRAME WITH
BLENDED PASTEL COLORS TO CREATE A
LOVELY CANVAS THAT DISPLAYS A FAVORITE
PHOTO, SEASHELLS, AND PEARL BEADS.

# CLever candle Trio

## WHaT YOU'LL need

Newspapers; glass candleholders; candles

Spray primer, such as KILZ

Acrylic enamel paints for glass, such as
Liquitex Glossies, in desired colors

Paintbrushes, including fine liner
and soft flat

Cotton ball; rubbing alcohol

Candle painting medium

## Here's HOW

**1** In a well-ventilated work area, cover the work surface with newspapers. Spray each of the candleholders with one or two light coats of primer, allowing to dry between coats. Let the last coat dry.

**2** Paint the candleholders with acrylic enamel paints, applying different colors to each of the sections. Let the paint dry. Use a fine liner brush to embellish the sections with stripes, lines, or dots.

**3** For each candle, dip a cotton ball in rubbing alcohol and wipe the candle surface prior to painting.

**4** Mix equal parts of candle painting medium with paint to decorate candles. Paint stripes, squiggles, dots, or other simple motifs. To paint stripes, use a soft flat paintbrush. Paint dots by dipping a paintbrush handle in paint and gently dotting on the candle surface. Let the paint dry.

CREATE A SENSATIONAL CENTERPIECE
BY PAINTING SUPER-SIMPLE DESIGNS ON
TAPER CANDLES AND HOLDERS.

# Beautiful
## Heart
## vase

## WHAT YOU'LL NEED

Large glass vase

Painter's tape

Paper

Glass spray paint, such as Krylon Stained Glass, in red or other desired color

Sponge; water

Paintbrushes

Acrylic enamel paints for glass, such as Liquitex Glossies, in yellow, orange, green, pink, and black

Metallic gold permanent paint pen

[continued on page 44]

USE GLASS PAINTS AND ACRYLIC ENAMELS
TO ADORN A VASE THAT SHINES LIKE A
STAINED GLASS WINDOW.

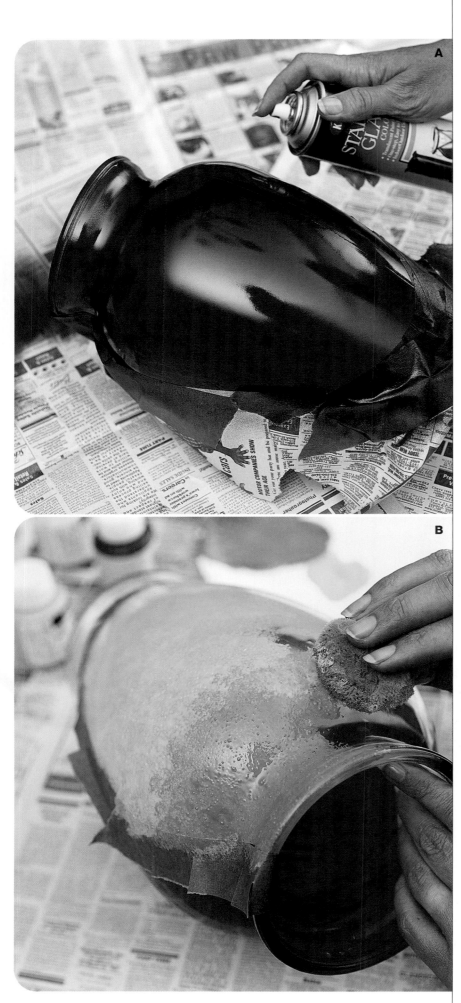

A

B

## Here's How

1 Wash and dry the vase. To create a random design on the vase, tape off areas with masking tape. Begin by placing tape onto glass to create a smooth line. Tape paper over the remaining large areas.

2 In a well-ventilated work area, practice spray painting by spraying paper. When comfortable with the application, spray-paint two to three light coats of red glass paint onto the taped-off area as shown in Photo A. Allow to dry between coats. Hold can at least 10 inches from the vase to prevent paint from running. Several light coats create a smoother finish. Let dry.

3 Cover the remaining areas of the vase with acrylic enamel paints. Soak a sponge in water and squeeze out the excess. For more texture, sponge a small amount of pink toward the top of the red sprayed area. Sponge yellow onto the next area. Blend in a small amount of orange toward the top as shown in Photo B.

c

4 Use a medium flat paintbrush to paint black lines between sections of painted areas. Let dry.

5 Referring to the pattern, *below,* paint a simple pink and orange heart in a green rectangle or any desired shape. The heart should overlap two painted areas; let dry. To make dots, dip the handle of a paintbrush into paint and dot onto the surface. Outline the motif with black. When all paint is dry, embellish black areas with a metallic gold paint pen as shown in Photo C.

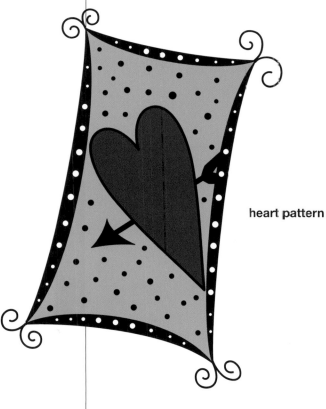

**heart pattern**

# Textured Treasures

## what you'll need

Candleholders

Masking tape; newspapers

Antique gold metallic textured paint, such as Krylon Fabulous Finishes Make It Stone!

Acrylic enamel paints, such as Liquitex Glossies, in teal, bright blue, black, and white

Disposable plate

Medium flat brush

Toothpick

Unpolished, smooth stones

## Here's How

1 Block off the painted areas of the candleholder with pieces of masking tape. Place the candleholder on newspapers in a well-ventilated work area. Spray two to three coats of metallic textured paint onto the candleholder, holding the can approximately 6 to 8 inches from the surface as shown in Photo A. The paint may come out chunky and appear uneven. Continue to

spray until the candleholder is covered, allowing a little drying time between coats. Let dry thoroughly. Remove the tape.

2 To create a turquoise look, place teal, bright blue, black, and white paints onto a plate. Dab a medium flat paintbrush in a generous amount of each color. Paint the candleholder areas where desired; avoid brushing back and forth and blending the colors together as shown in Photo B, *opposite*. Dip a toothpick into black and draw veins of black through thick wet paint as shown in Photo C. Let dry. Use the same technique to paint stones.

# WET PAINT
## MAKING THE MOST
### BEAUTIFUL WALLS

Your home is your castle and you deserve it to be magical. Surround yourself with all the colors and looks you love—like the glorious star-streaked galaxy, opposite or one of the innovative walls shown at right. Whether you want your home to have a natural ambience or want to drench it in the colors that make you smile, you're sure to find some beautiful treatments that reflect your personality. This chapter takes you step-by-step through four very different and very wall creative applications. The ones you choose will infuse your rooms with color and highlight your own personal magic.

# rainwashed wall

## WHAT YOU'LL NEED

Clear glaze

Good quality 3- or 4-inch paintbrush

Wall paints in olive green and turquoise

Color-washing brush

Spray bottle with water

Rag

[continued on page 52]

TOP COAT CLEAR GLAZE WITH WALL PAINTS AND SPRAY WITH WATER FOR MUTED, STREAKED SURROUNDINGS.

## Here's How

**1** Begin with clean dry white walls. Work on small sections of wall, ceiling to floor, that are easy to manage without letting the glaze dry. Paint the section with a generous coat of glaze using a good quality paintbrush as shown in Photo A. Do not let glaze dry.

**2** Immediately dab short strokes of olive green and turquoise paint into wet glaze as shown in Photo B.

**TEST THE COLORS AND TECHNIQUE ON GLAZED PLYWOOD BEFORE APPLYING ON A WALL.**

A

B

**3** Use a color-washing brush to gently merge the colors together in up and down strokes as shown in Photo C, until the wall is dotted with streaks of color. Avoid overblending. Colors should interlace yet remain distinguishable.

**4** Spray water onto the wall, beginning from the top and working downward as shown in Photo D. Experiment to get the desired effect. The more water used, the lighter the paint color will appear. Less water results in a stronger color of paint with less running. Set the spray bottle to spray a broad, even spray. Spray as much water as needed to get the paint to thin and run. Use the color-washing brush as necessary to reblend the paint. Keep a rag handy to dab excess paint water that pools at the bottom.

**5** Continue this process across the entire wall, always keeping a wet edge working from section to section.

C

D

# Leapin' Lizards

## What you'll need

Chalk line reel; tape measure

Roller with medium nap sleeve

Copper glaze; rubber combing tool

Latex wall paints in pale yellow, pale peach, and pink; paintbrush

Patterned double-headed roller

Double-welled paint pan

Rag roller sleeve

Decorative trim; turquoise acrylic paint

Small paintbrush for trim; rag

Rubber or plastic lizards

Newspapers; white spray primer

Acrylic enamel paints in turquoise, coral, and yellow

## Here's How

**1** Measure and mark off wall with chalk line where you want to divide the paint colors with moldings.

**2** Use a medium nap roller and yellow paint to cover such solid color areas as above the molding, *opposite*.

**3** Place equal amounts of pink and peach into each side of the double-welled paint pan. Coat the double-headed roller in a generous amount of paint and begin rolling onto the surface below the molding in random patterns working back and forth until covered as shown in Photo A. The more the roller is worked back and forth, the more the colors will blend. Less rolling results in

[continued on page 56]

TALK ABOUT A WALL WITH MOVEMENT! THIS PLAYFUL APPROACH INCLUDES A TRIO OF PAINTED LIZARDS CLIMBING ACROSS A BLENDED PAINT BACKDROP.

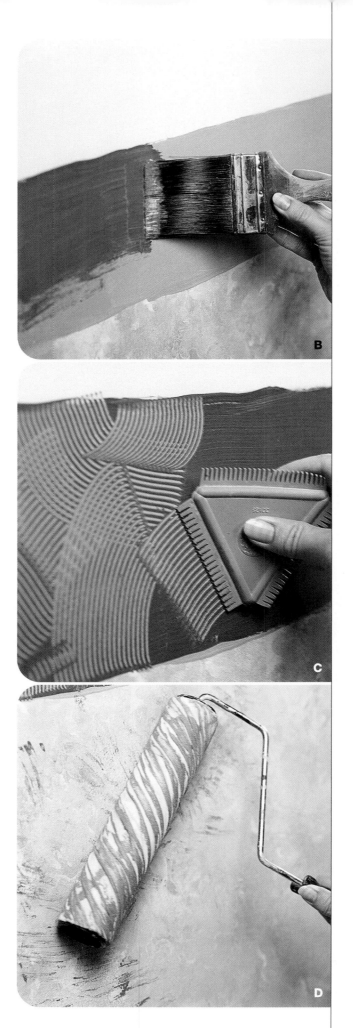

B

C

D

more distinct colors remaining. Experiment with the roller until familiar with how the paint applies to the wall.

**4** Use a wide brush to paint the narrow band of pink between the molding lines.

**5** Using a wide paintbrush, paint the copper glaze over the pink area as shown in Photo B. Use a generous amount of paint so the pink area is completely covered. While glaze is wet, use a rubber combing tool to rake in circular motions or desired designs as shown in Photo C. Let the glaze dry.

**6** Using a rag roller sleeve and copper glaze, roll glaze over the top and bottom sections of the wall as shown in Photo D.

**7** In a well-ventilated work area, cover the work surface with newspapers. Prime the trim; let dry. Paint the trim turquoise. Let the paint dry.

**8** Paint over turquoise with copper glaze as shown in Photo E. Use a damp rag to wipe off excess glaze as shown in Photo F. Let dry and attach to wall.

**9** In the ventilated work area, prime each of the lizards. Base-coat each lizard in a solid color; let dry. Paint stripes with a fine paintbrush or polka dots with the handle of a paintbrush. Layer dots with a contrasting color and smaller paintbrush, allowing to dry between coats. Use pins to attach lizards to the wall.

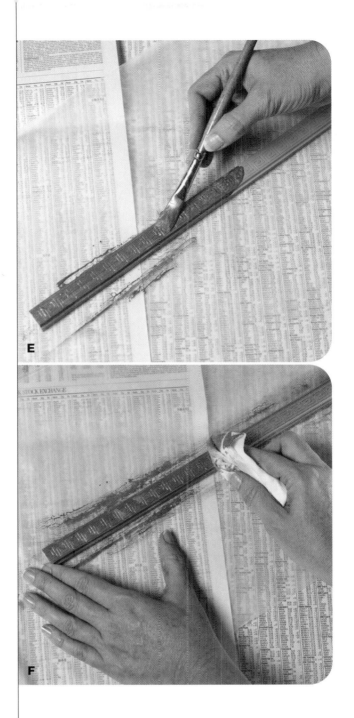

E

F

CHECK OUT TOY STORES FOR OTHER PLASTIC ACCENTS, SUCH AS LADYBUGS AND FROGS.

# CLEVER HANDWRITTEN BORDERS

## HERE'S HOW

Choose paints that blend together well and complement the color palette of the room. The colors pictured, *opposite,* are light purple, sea foam green, and cream. At left are pink, red, and white.

1 On paper, make a list of words to write on the wall. Arrange words so they vary in length, alternating short and long words.

2 Pour a small amount of each paint color on the plate. To practice painting, tape a piece of paper on the wall. Load the brush with all three colors of paint at the same time as shown in Photo A. Using your best penmanship, begin writing with paint, resting your hand on the wall as needed to steady the paintbrush. When comfortable with the process, begin painting on the wall. To correct a letter, quickly wipe off the area with a damp rag and let it dry before continuing.

## WHAT YOU'LL NEED

Latex wall paints in three desired colors

A small round paintbrush

Disposable plate

Paper

Tape

Rag

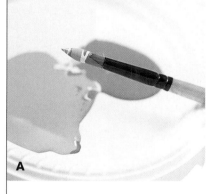

A

A FEW OF YOUR FAVORITE THINGS, PLACES YOU'VE TRAVELED. OR WHATEVER IS ON YOUR MIND—CHOOSE MEANINGFUL WORDS TO CREATE A MEMORABLE BORDER.

# moonLIGHT serenade

## WHAT YOU'LL NEED

### for the moon and planets

Tracing paper

Pencil

Heavy paper

Crafts knife

Sandpaper in coarse and medium grits

Circular plain toss toys, such as Frisbees, and plastic lids in assorted sizes

Spray paints in purple, black, red, orange, and yellow

Newspaper

Acrylic paint in dark red and yellow

Yellow marking pen

Toothbrush

[continued on page 62]

## WHAT YOU'LL NEED

### for the star wall

Blue wall paint

Roller pan

Roller with medium nap sleeve

Disposable plate

White acrylic paint

Water

Newspapers

Star-shape sponge roller pad, available at paint and crafts stores

BASK IN THE MOONLIGHT! USE TOSS TOYS AND PLASTIC LIDS TO TRANSFORM YOUR WALL INTO AN IMAGINATIVE GALAXY.

A

B

C

## here's how

**1** For the star wall, paint the wall solid blue. Let the paint dry.

**2** On a disposable plate, mix one part white acrylic paint and two parts blue wall paint. Thin with water to a light cream consistency. It should be thin enough to paint on transparently without running on the wall.

**3** On newspapers, practice rolling paint with a star sponge roller pad to get the desired effect. Roll back and forth in a smooth sweeping motion. Continue to roll until the roller runs out of paint. As you roll, the paint becomes thinner and a subtle effect is achieved. Continue rolling stars on wall until desired area is covered. Let dry.

**4** For the moon and planets, follow the same technique for all toss toys and lids, varying the colors and the order in which the paint colors are applied.

**5** Trace face pattern, *page 65,* onto tracing paper. Transfer onto heavy paper and cut out using a crafts knife. Set aside.

**6** Using coarse sandpaper, sand any raised areas on the toss toys or lids, such as lettering or designs. Follow with a medium grit paper. The surface may remain slightly uneven. Several layers of paint will smooth it out.

**7** In a well-ventilated work area, randomly spray black and purple until the toss toy is covered as shown in Photo A, *opposite.* It is fine if the paint runs during this step. Let the paint dry.

**8** Spray a generous layer of red over the dry purple and black as shown in Photo B. While the red paint is wet, spray the top portion of the toy orange as shown in Photo C. Quickly spray the edges black. Spray in a circular motion along the edge of the toy. While the paint is wet, crumple a piece of newspaper, press onto the wet paint, and lift off as shown in Photo D. Repeat this process over the entire toss toy, allowing all colors to be exposed. If less paint is pulling off then desired, repeat steps 7 and 8 as the paint may have dried between layers.

**9** Lightly highlight the top portion with yellow as shown in Photo E.

**10** Make a crater stencil from paper by cutting a dime, a nickel, and a quarter size hole in it. Hold the stencil about 2 inches from the toss toy and lightly spray through the holes with black paint held approximately 4 inches from the stencil as shown in Photo F.

[continued on page 64]

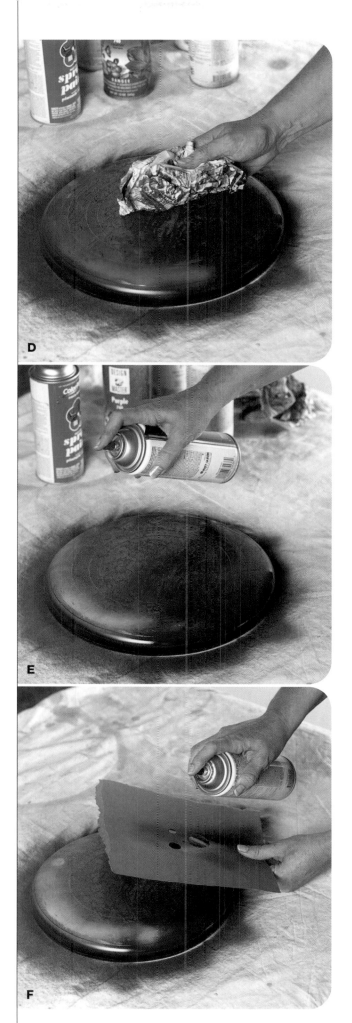

Spray these random circles on the lower dark portion. Do the same with yellow paint in the upper portion of the toss toy, continuing to spray lightly for a subtle effect.

**11** Spray the lower portion of the toss toy with a dark shadow of black as shown in Photo G. Let the paint dry.

**12** To practice painting the face, place the heavy paper template onto a piece of newspaper. Lightly spray yellow paint from at least 6 inches to apply very little color. When the desired look is achieved, place the template on the toss toy and paint as shown in Photo H. Let the paint dry.

**13** Thin the dark red acrylic paint until it is transparent. Paint in eyeballs. Let dry.

**14** Detail the facial features using a yellow paint pen as shown in Photo I.

**15** As shown in Photo J, splatter wet yellow acrylic paint on the top portion of the toss toy using a toothbrush. Flex bristles with finger to splatter. Let the paint dry.

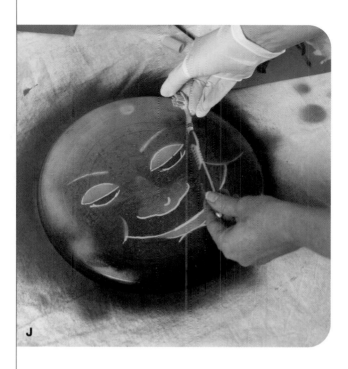

J

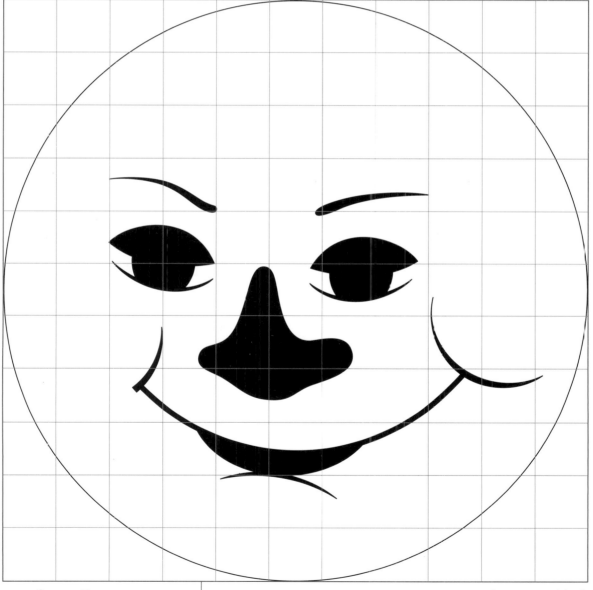

**moon face pattern**

**1 square = 1 inch**

# prideful FLIGHT SILHOUETTE

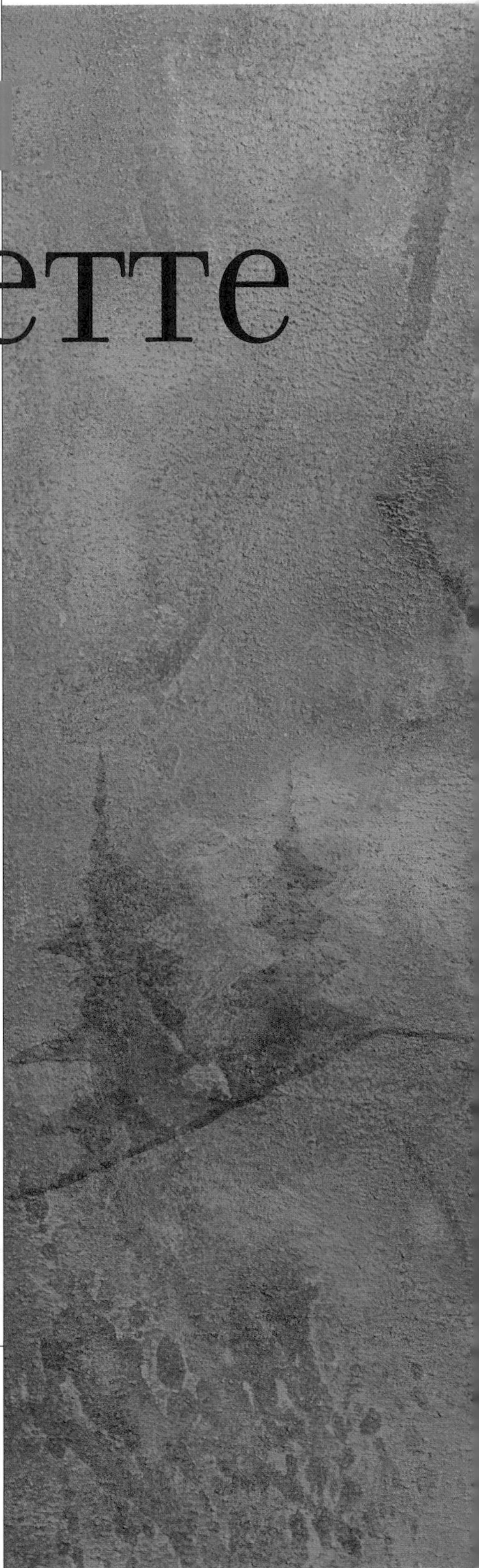

## what you'll need

Spray bottle with water; rags

Ocher acrylic or latex paint
(a quart of latex or several small bottles of acrylic)

Good quality 3- or 4-inch wall paintbrush

Crafts glazes in dark green, plum, dark burgundy,
and burnt umber

Large flat artist's paintbrush; badger brush

Rubber gloves; protective eye goggles

Denatured alcohol

Enlarged copy of pattern, page 71

Scissors; tape

Tracing paper; pencil

[continued on page 68]

A HANDSOME LOOK FOR TEXTURED OR FLAWED WALLS, THIS ARTISTIC TECHNIQUE OFFERS RUSTIC APPEAL.

## here's HOW

This technique works well on textured or sand-finished walls, although it also works on smooth walls. It even can be applied to walls with many flaws due to its rugged look. It requires little paint because the paint is thinned. Working continuously on a wet wall is important to achieve good results. *Read through all steps before beginning.*

**1** Work on one large section of wall at a time from top to bottom. It is important to keep a wet edge, so work only in as large an area as manageable. Spray the entire section with water so that it is evenly soaked. Use a rag to wipe up excess water frequently from bottom of wall, especially if it builds up and pools.

WORK CONTINUOUSLY ON A WET WALL TO ACHIEVE GOOD RESULTS.

**2** Dab random broad strokes of ocher color onto the wet wall as shown in Photo A, *opposite*. Spray small bursts of water onto areas to blend colors. Continue to dab off pooling water and excess paint with a rag.

**3** Use a large artist's brush to apply random strokes of glazes with green, burgundy, plum, and burnt umber as shown in Photo B.

**4** Use a badger brush to soften and blend the colors as shown in Photo C. The brush should remain as dry as possible. Use it lightly to remove extra wet paint and blend the colors. Use the brush to push paint into dark areas and wipe paint away from the lighter areas. Continually wipe off brush on a rag. Rinse out, dry, and fluff up brush if too much color accumulates in it. Avoid overblending colors.

**5** As the wall is drying but still damp to the touch, put on rubber gloves and goggles, dip fingers into denatured alcohol, and splatter on damp wall as shown in Photo D.

[continued on page 70]

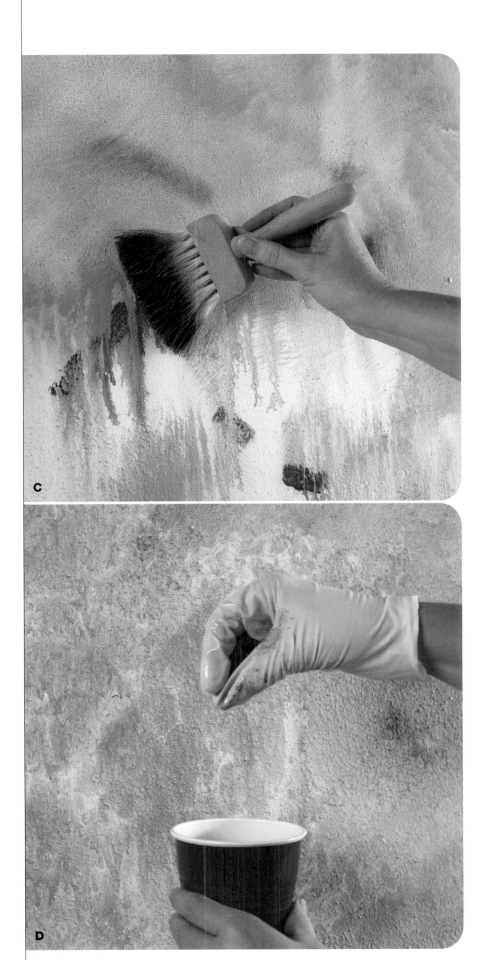

C

D

**6** When wall is nearly dry, use a clean rag to gently dab and wipe areas where alcohol was applied as shown in Photo E. This should remove paint, resulting in an aged, faded, stonelike look.

**7** Use a photocopier to enlarge the eagle pattern, *opposite,* to the desired size, piecing it together in sections if necessary. Cut out the eagle, tape it to wall, and trace around it lightly with a pencil.

**8** Use small amounts of plum and dark green glazes to paint in eagle shape as shown in Photo F. Dot on dabs of random color and blend together to fill in the eagle silhouette. Let the paint dry.

E

F

SPLATTER THE WALL WITH DENATURED ALCOHOL TO ENHANCE THE INTERESTING BACKGROUND.

eagle pattern

# CHOOSE your PALETTE
## coloring your great outdoors

Share your painting talent with family and friends by making colorful projects for the outdoors. This extraordinary chapter includes extra-easy planters that burst with color, a lovely picnic table graced with designs reminiscent of Norwegian rosemaling, and a playhouse that all children dream about. With more than a dozen projects to inspire your love of painting, the hard part is choosing which one to do first—a really cool tire swing for the kids...or a potting bench or lounge chair for you!

# FLOWer urn Trio

## WHaT YOU'LL need

Plastic urns
(available in discount stores
and home improvement
centers)

Newspapers

Spray paint for plastic,
such as Krylon's Fusion, in
burgundy, red, yellow, purple,
and blue

[continued on page 76]

SPRAY-PAINT
A TRIO OF
PLANTERS AND FILL
WITH BLOOMS FOR
A COLOR-RICH
PATIOSCAPE.

A

B

## Here's How

**1** Wash and dry the plastic urns. If the bowl piece comes apart from the base, separate the sections. Avoid touching the areas to be painted.

**2** In a well-ventilated work area, cover the work surface with newspapers. Place the urn sections on the newspaper, positioning them so the areas to be painted are facing up and the pieces are spread apart enough to control the paint coverage.

**3** If recommended by the paint manufacturer, shake the cans of spray paint to mix thoroughly. To apply a smooth, even coat and avoid running, spray light coats, holding paint can approximately 10 inches from the surface when spraying. Start with the darkest paint color and work to the lightest. For the red urn, start with dark blue, spraying the bowl rim, bowl bottom, and bottom edge of the base. Slightly overlap the colors, applying burgundy and red as shown in Photos A and B, *left*. For the yellow urn, start with red and highlight with yellow. For the blue urn, start with purple and finish with blue.

**4** If necessary, touch up areas with the appropriate color of spray paint. Allow the paint to dry 24 hours. Carefully reassemble the urns.

ACHIEVE A MORE VINTAGE LOOK. BASE-COAT THE URN WITH BLACK AND HIGHLIGHT WITH SUCH MUTED TONES AS OLIVE OR TAN.

# norwegian-
## STYLE
# PICNIC TABLE

## WHAT YOU'LL NEED

Sandpaper; paint stripper, if necessary

Wood picnic table

Tack cloth

Spray primer; newspapers

3-inch paintbrush

Acrylic paints in black, yellow, pale yellow, gold, medium blue, white, orange, and red

Satin acrylic house paints in black and medium blue

Crackle medium

Tracing paper; pencil

Transfer paper

Disposable plate

Artist's paintbrushes

Spray polyurethane varnish

[continued on page 80]

CAPTURE THE OLD-WORLD LOOK
OF ROSEMALING ON A CRACKLE-FINISH
TABLETOP.

79

## Here's How

1 Prepare the picnic table by sanding any rough spots. If necessary, strip the picnic table to allow it to be primed. Wipe away dust using a tack cloth.

2 In a well-ventilated work area, cover the work surface with newspapers. Place the picnic table on the newspapers and spray the table with a coat of primer. Let dry. Apply a second coat if needed. Sand the primer if needed and wipe away dust using a tack cloth.

3 Paint the tabletop with black acrylic paint as shown in Photo A. Paint the benches and other remaining portions using black house paint. Let the paint dry.

4 For the benches and bottom sections of the table, use blue and black house paint to achieve a highlighted look. Dip the 3-inch paintbrush into both paint colors and stroke the surface as shown in Photo B; avoid overblending. Continue painting in this manner until the benches and bottom sections of the table are covered. Let dry.

5 Paint a thick coat of crackle medium on the top of the picnic table as shown in Photo C. Let dry.

**6** Pour yellow, pale yellow, and gold paints on a plate. Without mixing, dip the 3-inch brush into the paints and apply a thin coat of paint over the crackle medium without brushing back and forth as shown in Photo D, *right.* Cover the entire tabletop and edges using the three colors. Let the paint crackle as it dries.

**7** Enlarge and trace the pattern, *pages 82–83.* Using transfer paper, transfer the design to the center of the tabletop. Using the pattern as a guide, paint the design with artist's brushes, blending colors as shown on *page 78.* Let the paint dry. Use yellows, blue, and white to make painted swirl and leaf designs on the benches and table legs as shown in Photo E and in the photos on *pages 78–79.* Let dry.

**8** Apply a coat of varnish to the entire table; let dry. Apply a second coat if needed and let dry.

**USE THIS TECHNIQUE ON LAWN FURNITURE, FENCES, BIRDHOUSES, OR OTHER OUTDOOR WOOD SURFACES.**

**top of picnic table rosemaling pattern**

**1 square = 1 inch**

# sunburst swing

## WHAT YOU'LL need

Newspapers

Clean, dry tire

3- or 4-inch wall paintbrush

Wide artist's brush

Medium round artist's brush

Outdoor acrylic enamel paints in purple, red, and yellow

## Here's HOW

**1** Cover work surface with newspapers. Lay tire on newspapers. Paint entire tire purple using a wide wall paintbrush; use an artist's brush to fill in the treads. Let dry. Turn tire over to paint the other side. Let dry.

**2** Draw curved ray shapes with red paint using a medium round brush and fill in the sections with red. Let dry.

**3** Highlight one edge with yellow using the medium round brush. Let dry.

HANG A HINT OF SUNSHINE IN YOUR
BACKYARD BY PAINTING COLORFUL RAYS
ON A KID-FRIENDLY TIRE SWING.

# GLORIOUS GARDEN BENCH

## WHAT YOU'LL NEED

Primer paint; paintbrushes

Wood bench

Self-contained stencil with no overlays

Stencil adhesive; trowel

All-purpose joint compound

Sponge; latex or acrylic paints in desired colors

[continued on page 88]

PLANT ANOTHER "FLOWER" IN YOUR
GARDEN—A BEAUTIFUL YET PRACTICAL
BENCH WITH RAISED STENCIL MOTIFS.

**A**

**B**

## here's HOW

1 Paint a coat of primer on the surface of the bench. Let it dry.

2 Apply stencil adhesive to the stencil and position it on the surface to be painted.

3 Trowel on joint compound evenly to approximately ⅛ inch thickness over the stencil as shown in Photo A.

4 Starting at any corner, lift the stencil slowly until completely removed as shown in Photo B.

REMOVE THE STENCIL WHILE THE JOINT COMPOUND IS WET TO REVEAL A RAISED DESIGN.

**C**

**USE AN ARTIST'S PAINTBRUSH TO CAREFULLY PAINT AROUND THE RAISED DESIGNS.**

**D**

**E**

5  Allow joint compound to dry thoroughly.

6  Sponge surface with a damp sponge to remove rough edges as shown in Photo C, *opposite*. Let dry.

7  Prime the raised designs and let dry.

8  Paint the flat background the desired color as in Photo D. Paint the raised stencil design with desired colors as shown in Photo E. Let dry. Paint the details of the bench using the desired colors.

# WOOD-GRAINED POTTING BENCH

## WHAT YOU'LL NEED

Light satin or semi-gloss
base coat latex paint

Paintbrush; potting bench

Dark satin or semi-gloss
top coat latex paint in
desired colors

Wood-graining tool

Water-based faux finish
glaze; 1-inch-wide
painter's tape; varnish

[continued on page 92]

GET A HEAD START ON GARDEN CHORES
WITH THIS CLASSY POTTING BENCH.

A

B

## Here's how

1 Base-coat the potting bench with paint. Let dry.

2 Mix the top coat with faux finish glaze, one part paint to three parts glaze. Brush the glaze mixture generously on the potting bench as shown in Photo A.

3 Put the bottom edge of the graining tool onto the surface of the bench where graining is desired. Pull the tool toward you and rock it back and forth as shown in Photo B. Rocking faster produces smaller wood grain patterns; rocking slower produces larger, longer patterns. The patterns can be made without lining up strokes; however, if an area lacks the desired look, pick up the tool and go over it. Let dry.

**C**

4 To create a lattice effect, place tape strips in a crisscross pattern. Use a stencil brush to dab paint between the tape strips as shown in Photo C. Let the paint dry and remove the tape. Paint the remaining parts of the bench as desired. Let dry.

5 Coat the potting bench with varnish to seal and protect the bench. Let the varnish dry.

# fresh
# air
# focus

## WHAT YOU'LL NEED

### for the chairs

Chairs; primer, if needed

Acrylic enamel paints in purple and pink

Paintbrush; sealer

Combing tool (available at crafts and paint stores)

[continued on page 96]

GRAB AN ICED TEA OR LEMONADE
AND REJUVENATE WHILE ENJOYING THIS
DELIGHTFUL PATIO SET.

A

B

## HERE'S HOW

**1** Prime the chairs if needed; let dry. Paint the chairs purple; let dry.

**2** Paint the flat sections of the chair pink. While wet, comb through the paint to reveal the base coat as shown in Photo A. Let dry.

**3** Apply two or three coats of sealer to entire chair; let dry.

## WHAT YOU'LL NEED

**for the umbrella**

Plain canvas umbrella

White gesso, available at crafts and art stores

Tracing paper; pencil

Paintbrush; acrylic enamel paints in purple and pink

Polyurethane or sealer

## HERE'S HOW

**1** Paint the umbrella top with gesso; let dry.

**2** Trace the petal pattern, *opposite*, enlarging to fit umbrella; cut out. Trace onto umbrella. Paint the petals purple and blend in pink as shown in Photo B.

**3** Paint highlights and the flower center with pink. Create purple dots in the flower center using the paintbrush handle. Let dry. Apply two coats of sealer over the top of the umbrella.

flower petal pattern

# PLAYFULLY COOL PLAYHOUSE

## HERE'S HOW

Dress up any simple structure to make it look like this gingerbread house. Use a warm gingerbread color of paint for the exterior and white for trim. Cut simple heart shapes from wood (patterns, *page 107*) and paint pink. Paint subtle highlights in hearts by adding a stroke of white into the wet pink paint. The stars shown, *opposite,* are simple plastic foam stars screwed onto the exterior. A scalloped trim gives the look of icing.

**1** Purchase enough pipe to extend down from each corner of the house.

**2** Measure and cut each piece to fit exactly.

**3** Start with clean, white pipe. Sand off any markings with medium grit sandpaper.

**4** Wind wide masking tape around pipe at an

[continued on page 100]

## WHAT YOU'LL NEED

### for the exterior

Paints for exterior; wood for hearts; tracing paper; pencil
Scissors; acrylic paints in pink and white; scroll saw

4-inch diameter PVC pipe for corners

Medium grit sandpaper

Wide masking tape; red spray paint; saber saw

Screws and screw gun for attaching pipes

CREATE A GETAWAY FOR THE KIDS THAT'S AS SWEET AS ONE IN A FAIRY TALE. DON'T FORGET THE GINGERBREAD TOUCHES!

angle. Continue winding evenly until the pipe is covered.

**5** Spray the pipe using red spray paint as shown in Photo A. Let dry. Spray another coat if necessary. Let dry and remove tape.

**6** Measure and mark two vertical lines from top to bottom to define section to be cut from pipe. Section will fit onto corners.

**7** Use a saber saw to cut out pipe section. Use screws and screwgun to fit onto corners of house.

## WHAT YOU'LL NEED

### for the interior

Latex wall paints in lavender and pink

Paintbrush; large sponge

Tracing paper; pencil; water

Scissors; heavy paper; ruler

Crafts knife; masking tape

Stencil cream paints in white, green, and pale lavender; stencil brushes

Gold paint pen

## HERE'S HOW

**1** Begin with clean, primed walls. Paint the ceiling solid lavender.

**2** Work wall in sections to always keep a wet edge. Paint a large area using pink. Stop short of the ceiling where the two colors will blend. Paint dabs of lavender and pink in the area to be blended as in Photo B, *opposite*.

**3** Soak a sponge in water, squeeze out excess, and sponge the lavender and pink to blend the two together as shown in Photo C, *opposite*. Blend from top to bottom, sponging the lavender fading into the pink.

**4** Enlarge and trace stencil shapes, *pages 106–107,* onto tracing paper. Cut out and trace onto heavy paper. Cut out with crafts knife, keeping both window frame and cutout shapes intact. Save cutout shapes for later use. For window trim, measure so the heart stencil is centered above window and level. Tape stencil frame onto wall.

**5** Using white stencil cream and a large stencil brush, apply cream in a firm circular motion as shown in Photo D. Continue until well covered; let dry. If more intense color is desired, apply a second coat. Create leaves for window trim in the same manner using green stencil cream. Let dry.

**6** Tape the heart cutout shape onto the stenciled area, covering the painted shape. Use a small stencil brush and lavender paint, as shown in Photo E, to dab a shadow

[continued on page 102]

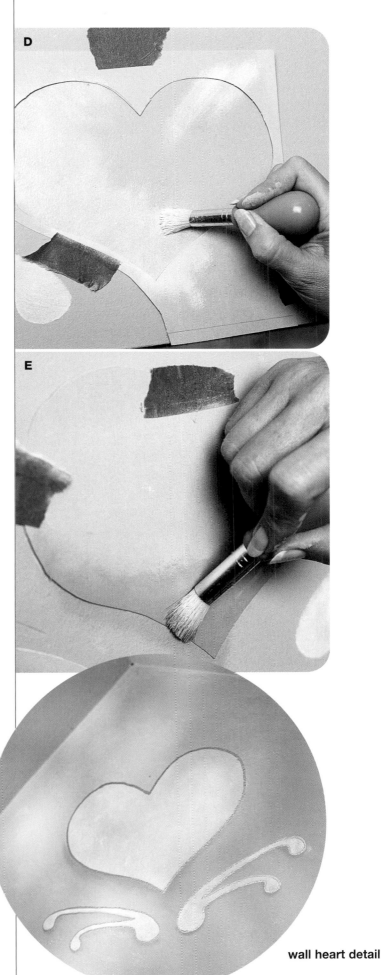

**wall heart detail**

101

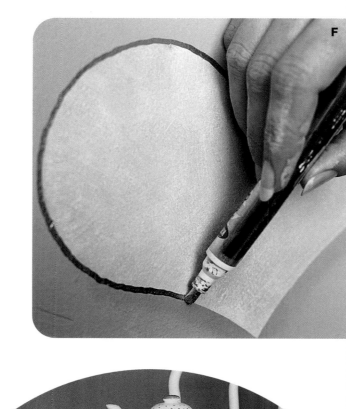

F

under each leaf, swirl, and heart. Stencil about a ½-inch shadow under each piece. Let dry.

**7** Outline shapes using gold paint pen as shown in Photo F.

## WHAT YOU'LL NEED

**for the toddler table**

Small decorative table

White spray primer, such as KILZ

Acrylic paints in lavender, pink, green, and white

Medium and wide flat artist's paintbrushes

Clear-coat sealer

## HERE'S HOW

**1** Begin with clean, dry piece. Spray two light, even coats of primer, allowing to dry between coats.

**2** Paint larger, solid color areas first, such as lavender sections. Use a wide, flat brush. Apply paint smoothly and quickly while paint is still wet. Before lavender paint dries, clean brush, dip in white, and stroke highlights in raised areas leaving the recessed areas the deeper tone. Paint different sections of the legs different colors, using a medium brush. Paint smaller sections between colors with white. Finish with clear-coat sealer.

## WHAT YOU'LL NEED

### for the rug

Acrylic paints in lavender and pink

Fabric painting medium

Disposable plate

Rug

Flat paintbrush

## HERE'S HOW

**1** Mix one part fabric painting medium with two parts acrylic paint, mixing a few tablespoons at a time on a plate.

**2** Paint alternating lavender and pink stripes onto rug using a flat fabric brush. The pictured chenille rug is very textured, so it requires a good amount of paint to soak in. Use the paint generously and brush firmly into the fibers. Let dry.

[continued on page 104]

CHOOSE A RUG WITH A DEFINED TEXTURE TO USE AS A PAINTING GUIDE FOR A COORDINATED LOOK.

## WHAT YOU'LL need

### for the tea set and napkin

White ceramic tea set

Acrylic gloss enamels or glass paints appropriate for food utensils in green and other desired colors

Sponge; water; paper

Foam dotter; paintbrush

Acrylic paints in lavender and pink

Fabric painting medium

Disposable plate

Cloth napkin

½-inch-wide flat paintbrush

## Here's HOW

**1** Begin with clean, dry tea set. Thin green paint with a little water to a light cream consistency. Soak sponge in water, squeeze out excess, and dab in a small amount of green. Test on paper first. Sponge a little paint on so it appears transparent. Lightly sponge on front of cups and teapot or wherever you wish. Let dry.

**2** To paint flowers, dip foam dotter in lavender and pink paint and press onto surface. For smaller flowers, dip a paintbrush handle in paint and dot onto surface. Let dry. Use paintbrush to make green leaves. Paint stripes on handles, alternating colors.

**3** Follow the paint manufacturer's instructions if they require baking to set the paint.

### for the napkin

**1** Mix one part fabric painting medium to two parts acrylic paint on a disposable plate; mix quarter-size amounts at a time.

**2** On a clean, pressed napkin, use a fabric paintbrush to paint alternating stripes around the edge of napkin. Let dry.

# WHAT YOU'LL NEED

## for the chairs

Ice-cream chairs

White spray primer, such as KILZ

Masking tape

White spray paint

Acrylic enamels in lime green, pink, purple, blue gray, and white

Wide and medium flat artist's paintbrushes

Foam dotters ¼- and ½-inch in diameter

Tracing paper

Pencil

Scissors

# HERE'S HOW

**1** Begin with clean, dry chairs. Spray two light even coats of primer over the entire chair. Allow to dry between coats.

**2** Cover seat area with masking tape. Spray two to three light even coats of white spray paint onto chairs. Allow to dry between coats of paint.

**3** Paint the background colors of seats first. Paint the green or lavender background using a wide flat artist's brush. Let dry and paint a second coat if needed.

**4** To make the dotted chair, dip the foam tip of the ½-inch dotter into paint and apply random dots of blue gray to the chair seat. Let dry.

**5** Stamp different colors over the blue gray dots, offsetting the color slightly to leave a shadow of blue gray. Let dry.

**6** To make the checkered chair, draw squiggle line patterns onto tracing paper. Cut out and tape onto chair in a checkerboard pattern. Trace with pencil.

[continued on page 106]

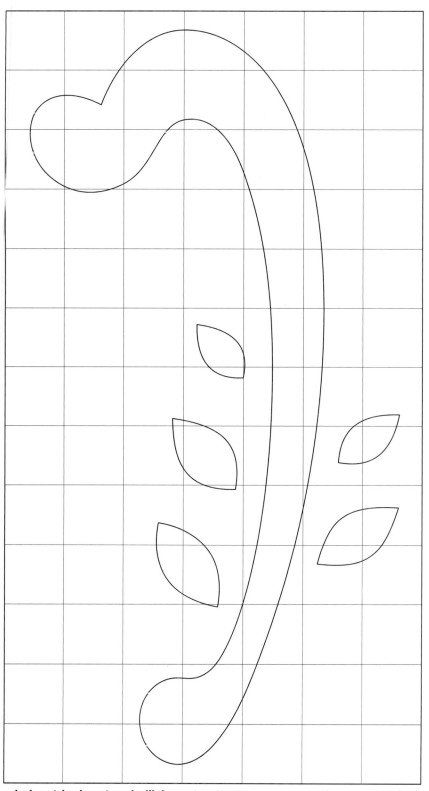

**window trim heart embellishment pattern**      **1 square = 1 inch**

7 Paint the squiggle lines gray using a flat paintbrush. Let dry. Paint the same squiggle shape in white over top of the gray line to create a shadow, using the gray line as a guide and offsetting the white as was done for the dots. Make sure the shadows all end up offset equally, either on bottom and left or top and right of white lines.

8 To make flowers, use the same technique. Use the foam dotter to paint a series of gray dots in a flower shape. Paint gray leaves. Let dry. Paint the colored flowers and leaves over top of the gray. Again make sure the shadow appears consistent with the rest of the shadows. Let chairs dry at least 24 hours before using.

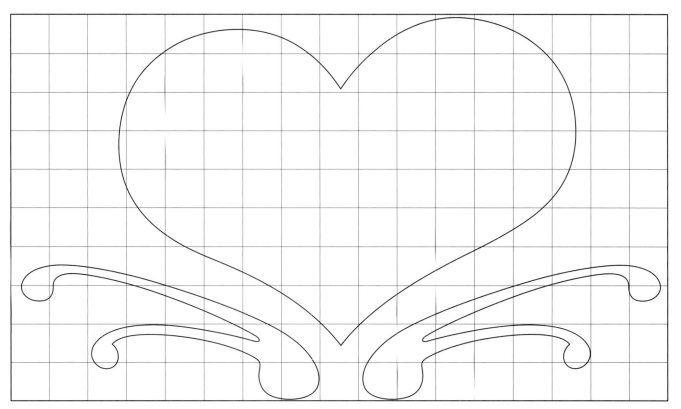

**wall heart pattern**

**1 square = 1 inch**

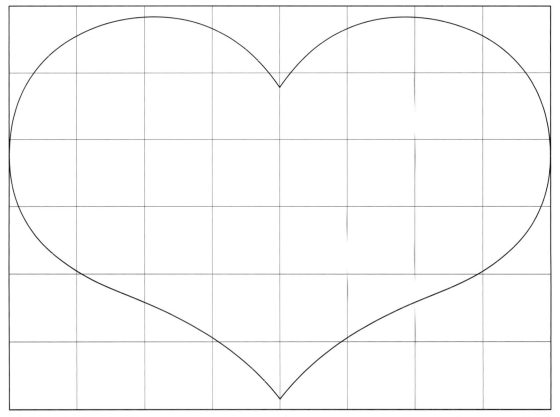

**window trim heart pattern**

**1 square = 1 inch**

# RAGS TO riches

## PAINTING FLEA MARKET FINDS

The greatest sense of accomplishment comes from taking someone else's "junk" and turning it into a gem. This chapter shows you how to meet the challenge using artistic techniques for painting fabric, wood furniture, glassware, and ceramics. Choose the look that complements you—contemporary, Victorian, traditional—the chapter covers them all. Then get out paint in your favorite hues, select a flea market castaway, and begin the transformation. You'll create a treasure you can give away with pride or one you'll want to keep forever.

# TIMELY TABLE

## WHAT YOU'LL NEED

Table

Paint stripper and sandpaper, if necessary

Stain; wood varnish

Metallic acrylic paints, such as Createx, in pink, lime green, red, yellow, purple, and turquoise

Medium flat and round paintbrushes

## HERE'S HOW

**1** Prepare table surface for painting. Strip off finish and sand if necessary. Stain and varnish areas that will remain unpainted.

**2** To paint solid color areas, use a small or medium flat brush. Use narrow brushes to paint the finer sections of wood. To blend such colors as yellow and pink, paint a section pink. Paint the section next to it yellow. While still wet, blend the two colors together. Let the paint dry.

**3** To paint dots, dip the handle of the paintbrush into paint and dot onto surface. Let the paint dry.

PAINT PIZZAZZ ON A FLEA MARKET TABLE
BY TRANSFORMING THE EDGES AND DETAILS
WITH VIVID METALLIC PAINTS.

# pretty Peach Dresser

## Here's HOW

**1** Take out the drawers and remove pulls from drawers. Begin with clean, dry, prepared surface, sanding or stripping the dresser as necessary. Wipe off dust with a tack cloth. In a well-ventilated work area, cover the work surface with newspapers. Lightly spray primer onto surfaces to be painted. Let dry. Spray second coat if necessary. Let dry.

**2** Paint the entire dresser cream using a wide flat paintbrush. Let dry. Paint on more coats if necessary, allowing the paint to dry between coats.

[continued on page 114]

## What you'll need

Dresser; sandpaper, paint stripper, and tack cloth if needed

Newspapers; white spray primer, such as Kilz

Acrylic paints in cream, coral, soft marigold yellow, peach, olive green, and metallic gold

Round and small, medium, and wide flat paintbrushes

Large stencil brush; brown stencil cream

Tracing paper; soft lead pencil; tape; disposable plate

Clear satin sealer

**before**

GIVE AN OLD DRESSER A
PEACHES-AND-CREAM COMPLEXION
USING A VARIETY OF PAINTS
AND BRUSHES.

**10** To paint leaves use various shades of all these colors. Paint each leaf differently. To create shape in the leaves, it is important to have contrast of light, medium, and dark tones as shown in Photo F, *page 115*. The tones can vary from light green to deeper green or to a more brown or pink color. To make lighter sections of leaves, mix more cream or yellow to the color mixture.

**11** Make small dots of metallic gold around peach and leaves. Dip handle of small paintbrush in gold paint and dot onto surface. Let dry.

**12** Seal with a clear satin sealer. Let dry.

**leaves drawer patterns**

**peach and leaves drawer patterns**          **1 square = 1 inch**

peach and leaves dresser
top right front and left back
corner patterns

peach and leaves dresser
top left front and right back
corner patterns

117

# TROPICAL STAND

## WHAT YOU'LL need

Unfinished nightstand or other desired furniture

Newspapers; spray primer, such as KILZ

Acrylic paints in black, dark blue-green, grass green, lime green, white, hot pink, orange, and yellow

Wide flat and fine artist's paintbrush

Silk or pressed dried, firm fern leaves, such as leatherleaf or other grass or plant, to use as stencils

Spray adhesive; sponge

Tracing paper; pencil; crafts knife; heavy paper

Cloth; black paint marker; glossy spray varnish

## Here's HOW

This technique is primarily three colors of green—dark, medium, and light—all blended and layered from the outer edges to the center. Always work from the edges inward, beginning with a dark color and finishing with light.

1 Begin with a clean, dry piece of furniture. Remove all hardware, such as handles and pulls, before painting.

2 In a well-ventilated work area, cover the work surface with newspapers. Spray two light and even coats of primer onto all surfaces of furniture, allowing to dry between coats. Let dry.

[continued on page 120]

**before**

118

MAKE A HO-HUM, GARAGE SALE ACCENT
TABLE SHINE BY STENCILING ELEGANT
RAIN FOREST MOTIFS.

119

**A**

**B**

ACCENT THE FURNITURE PIECE WITH THE VIBRANT COLORS USED TO PAINT THE BUTTERFLIES.

**C**

3 Paint furniture black; let dry. Paint a second coat if needed. Let dry.

4 Lightly spray one side of leaves with adhesive. Let dry. Test its tackiness on a smooth surface. It should be tacky enough to stick to it but able to be removed easily. If too tacky, press against a towel.

5 Arrange leaves and grass in a single layer around the outer edge as shown in Photo A. Wherever leaves are placed, black leaves will appear as if they are in a forest foreground.

6 Sponge along the outside edge with the dark blue-green paint as shown in Photo A. Also sponge this color around the edges covering about two-thirds of the outer edge of the leaves. Blend the grass green into the blue-green. Sponge and blend these colors together gradually with the lighter shade toward the center. Paint the entire piece with these two colors. Let dry.

7 Keep the original leaves in place and adhere another row of leaves toward the center as shown in Photo B. These leaves will remain the green shade just painted underneath.

8 Sponge on the grass green. starting over the area where the blue green blends into the grass green, but leaving the outer area

as is. Blend into the center with the lime green. Let dry.

9 When dry, use a clean, wet sponge to blot a few dabs of lime green in the center. Let dry.

10 Carefully remove the leaves as shown in Photo C, *opposite*. Use a paintbrush to redefine any shapes where paint seeped under the leaf.

11 Trace the butterfly pattern onto tracing paper, cut out, and trace onto heavy paper; cut out to create a stencil.

12 Tape butterfly stencil onto painted surface. Sponge the area with white acrylic paint as shown in Photo D. Let dry.

13 Hold stencil back in place over white area and sponge on hot pink and orange as shown in Photo E. Let dry. Paint the yellow butterfly in the same manner.

14 If desired, trim the furniture with contrasting details by quickly sponging on pink and orange, wiping any excess paint from the green areas with a damp cloth.

15 Outline butterflies and draw details with a black paint marker. Make detail lines in pink and orange trim. Let dry.

16 Spray on two coats of varnish, allowing to dry between coats. Let dry. Reattach hardware.

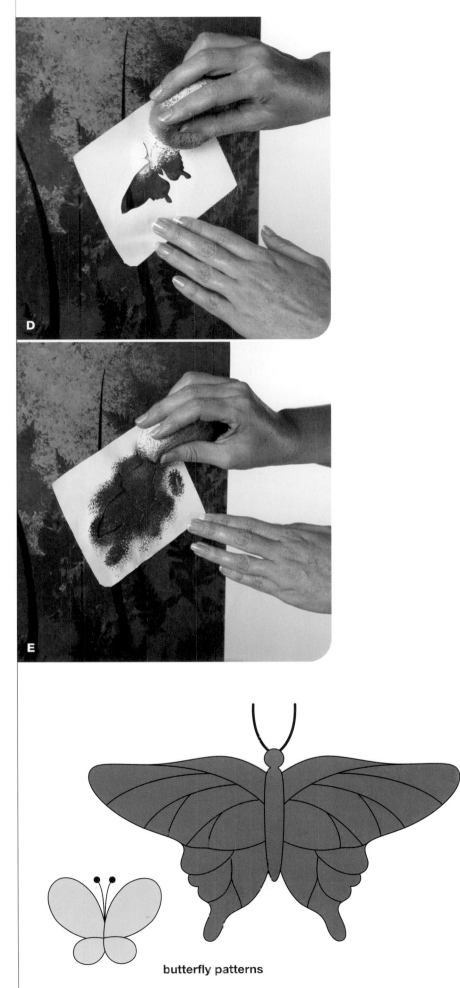

butterfly patterns

# color-Drenched sofa and ottoman

here's how

**here's HOW**

**1** Paint the ottoman with white latex wall paint using a roller or brush. Apply paint so that it works into the fibers without having excess on the surface. Let dry.

**2** If necessary, thin the acrylic paints to a light cream consistency. Paint entire piece with a thin coat of orange. Applying paint too thickly may result in cracking. Let dry.

**3** Use a flat paintbrush to apply hot pink over orange as shown in Photo A, *page 124*. Begin in one corner and fade paint toward center. Let dry.

[continued on page 124]

**before**

## WHaT YOU'LL Need

### for the ottoman

Upholstered ottoman

White latex wall paint

Medium nap paint roller or wide paintbrush

Acrylic paints in orange, hot pink, purple, green, lime green, yellow, black, and white

Small flat paintbrush; black paint marker

Tracing paper; pencil; scissors; masking tape

**before**

GIVE FABRIC FURNITURE A
VIBRANT FACELIFT WITH LAYERS
OF INTENSE COLOR.

**4** Trace flower pattern, *opposite,* onto tracing paper; cut out and tape in place on ottoman. Trace around it with a pencil.

**5** Paint flower purple and leaf green. Highlight green with lime green accents as shown in Photo B. To make yellow dots on flower and black dots along leaf, dip paintbrush handle in paint and dot surface. Let dry.

**6** Outline flower with black paint marker.

**7** To paint piping, line neatly with masking tape along each edge. Use a small flat brush to apply a coat of unthinned black paint as shown in Photo C, *opposite.* Make sure the paint is thick enough to avoid seeping under the masking tape when applying a light coat. Let dry.

**8** Use small flat paintbrush to paint white stripes. Let dry and remove masking tape.

JAZZ UP AN UPHOLSTERED OTTOMAN WITH A BOLDLY PAINTED POSY PLANTED ON ONE SIDE.

A

B

c

## WHAT YOU'LL NEED

**for the sofa**

Drop cloth

Clean upholstered sofa

Medium nap paint roller

Brush-on primer, such as latex wall paint*

Five to ten 4-ounce bottles of latex or acrylic paints for finishing fabric, such as Createx, in intense colors

Water spray bottle; artist's paintbrushes; black acrylic paint

## HERE'S HOW

*The primer coat should be similar in color to the final coat. Using similar colors saves paint on the final coat.*

[continued on page 126]

**ottoman flower pattern**

This technique works well for flea market furniture to cover stains or outdated or unwanted patterns. The finish feels like canvas and is somewhat crisp, making it an appropriate piece for a porch, garage, or rec room. Choose a sofa that has a fairly smooth texture with simple lines and is free of ruffles or puckers that make it difficult to paint.

1 In a well-ventilated work area, cover work surface with a drop cloth.

2 Remove sofa cushions. It is important to prime the fabric because when the first coat of paint soaks in, it creates a paintable canvas surface to hold the final coat of color. Prime light, bright colors with white or a light color and prime dark colors with a similar or medium-tone paint. Since this sofa will be pink and purple, it was primed with both white and purple latex paints. Prime the top of the couch with white. Paint the bottom area with purple. Roll the paint on firmly with a medium nap roller sleeve as shown in Photo D. Paint the purple right up to the white. Roll the paint on firmly and enough to cover it. Apply enough paint to cover and soak into fabric without forming puddles.

**3** Use a 3-inch wall paintbrush next to blend the white into the purple while it is still wet as shown in Photo E. You should see the texture of the fabric without seeing brush marks. Areas of heavy paint will crack when dry. Use the brush to even out any areas that have too much or too little paint. Let dry. This may take overnight.

**4** For the top coat, thin the paint to a light cream consistency, if necessary. Using a water spray bottle, spray a section of the sofa to allow the paint to go on and distribute evenly. Begin at the top of sofa section in the white area using a 3-inch wall brush. Paint pink downward and fade off beyond the point where the colors will blend as shown in Photo F. Paint the purple upward beginning from the bottom. Blend the two wet colors together, painting with horizontal strokes. Use the same technique to paint each remaining section. Let dry. If necessary, apply a second coat.

**5** Use a small brush to paint the piping carefully with black acrylic. Let dry.

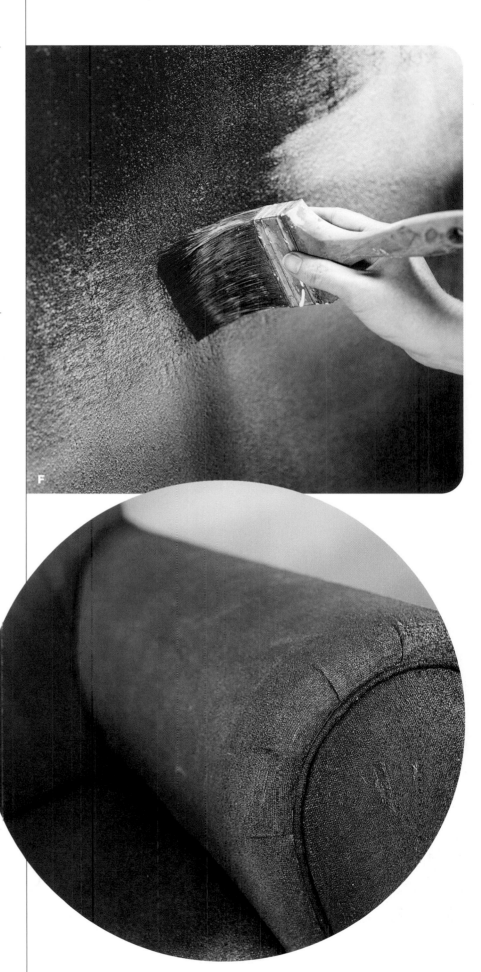

F

# STUDENT
# DESK

## WHAT YOU'LL NEED

School-style desk and chair

Masking tape

Newspapers

Spray primer, such as KILZ

Black spray paint

Paint markers in desired colors

## HERE'S HOW

**1** Begin with clean, dry desk. Mask off the areas to remain unpainted.

**2** In a well-ventilated work area, cover the work surface with newspapers. Spray a light coat of spray primer on the desk. Let dry. Repeat if needed.

**3** Spray two or three light, even coats of black spray paint on the desk, allowing to dry between coats. Let the final coat dry.

**4** Draw as many designs as desired to fill the surfaces using paint markers. Write words, draw shapes, or doodle dogs, cats, hearts, flowers, or other favorite motifs. Repeat geometric patterns around the edges. Let the paint dry.

ADORN A THRIFT STORE DESK WITH
PLAYFULLY DOODLED PAINT MARKER
GRAFFITI AND REPETITIVE DESIGNS.

# dainty
## pastel
## chair

**before**

## WHAT YOU'LL need

Chair prepared for painting

Masking tape; newspapers

Metallic gold spray paint

Wide paintbrush

Crackle medium

Acrylic paints in pink, lavender, cream, and green

Sponge; water; rag

Toothbrush; stick; clear spray varnish

## HERE'S HOW

1 Mask off areas to remain unpainted.

2 In a well-ventilated work area, cover the work surface with newspapers. Spray the chair with metallic gold paint; let dry.

[continued on page 132]

ENHANCE THE CHARM OF THIS
MUCH-LOVED CHAIR WITH A CRACKLED
COAT AND PAINTED DETAILS.

**A**

**B**

3 Apply two coats of crackle medium to areas of the chair where crackling is desired as shown in Photo A, allowing to dry between coats.

4 Mix pink paint with water to a consistency of very thin cream. It should be thin enough to crackle when painted over the crackle medium. Apply paint using strokes in one direction and without brushing back and forth as shown in Photo B. The crackle will appear as it dries. Let the paint dry.

5 Soak sponge in water and squeeze out excess. Dab sponge in one color of thinned paint, dab onto surface, sponge into another color, and press onto surface as shown in Photo C, *opposite.* Do this with as few and quick pats as possible, finishing the sponging before the paint dries. Avoid overworking paint with repeated dabs in areas that are crackled. Use a damp rag to quickly wipe off excess paint on desired areas to reveal gold paint.

6 Paint in other solid areas as desired. Let dry.

7 Spray a generous amount of gold paint into the head of a toothbrush. Brush a stick or other object against toothbrush to splatter gold paint onto the surface of chair. Let dry.

8 Spray entire chair with two or three light coats of clear varnish, allowing to dry in between coats. Let the final coat dry.

TO AVOID GETTING HANDS MESSY WHILE SPLATTERING PAINT, WEAR RUBBER GLOVES OR PLACE HANDS IN PLASTIC BAGS.

# stenciled Lace Table

## WHAT YOU'LL NEED

### for the table

Satin or eggshell finish interior latex paint in desired color for lace

2- or 3-inch wall paintbrush

1 or 2 vinyl lace tablecloths

Scissors

Stencil adhesive

[continued on page 136]

**before**

GIVE A BELOVED, OLD TABLE NEW LIFE
WITH ELEGANT STENCILS THAT LEND A
SPECIAL AMBIENCE TO DINING.

135

Towel

Well-used 2- or 3-inch natural hair paintbrush

Artist's paintbrushes

Semi-gloss interior latex paints in desired colors for table; paper plate or towel

1-inch-wide painter's tape

## Here's How

**1** Base-coat the table with satin finish paint in the desired color. Let the paint dry.

**2** Lay the tablecloth on the table with the points laying at the table edge. If necessary, use two cloths to cover the tabletop. If using two tablecloths, place them back to back, matching up the pattern as exactly as possible; trim where the tablecloths will butt together in the center of the table.

**3** Spray stencil adhesive on the back of the tablecloths, following the manufacturer's directions.

A

B

**4** Lay down one tablecloth on the table in the position desired. Bunch up a towel in both hands and press down hard all over the tablecloth until all air pockets are eliminated. Position the second tablecloth to butt against the edge of the first. Be careful to match patterns. Repeat the process with the towel on the second tablecloth.

**5** Dip the natural hair paintbrush in the top coat paint, blotting off the excess onto a paper plate or towel.

**6** Dab the natural hair paintbrush on the tablecloth, holding the brush straight up and down so the bristles do not slip under the stencil as shown in Photo A, *opposite*. Paint all solid table areas. Let the paint dry.

**7** Lift up the stencil and pull it back evenly until removed as shown in Photo B, *opposite*.

**8** Accent the table legs by masking off and painting the sections different colors as shown in Photo C using artist's paintbrushes. Add simple motifs if desired, as shown in Photo D.

[continued on page 138]

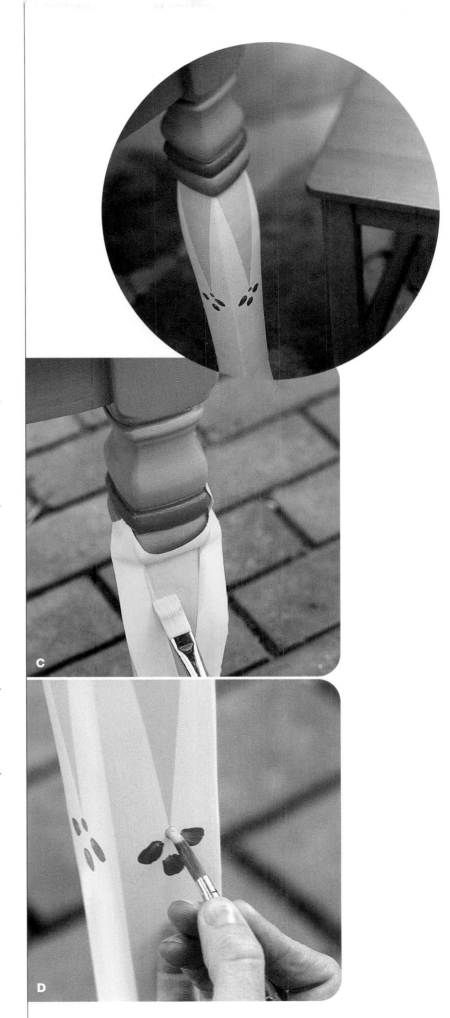

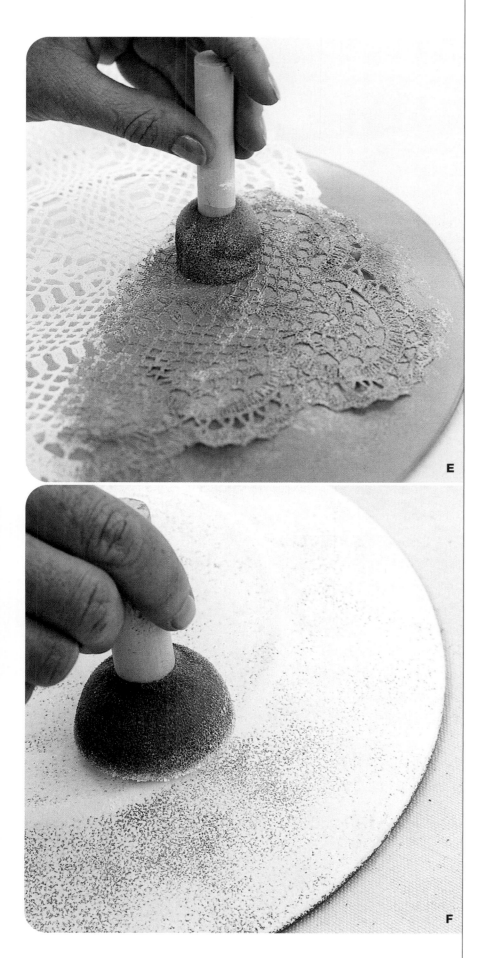

E

F

## WHAT YOU'LL NEED

### for the plates and vase

Clear glass plates; vase

Vinyl lace; scissors

Stencil adhesive

Painting sponge

Acrylic enamel glass paints, such as PermEnamel by Delta Ceramcoat, in olive, seafoam green, and cream

Clear gloss top coat

Paintbrush

## HERE'S HOW

1 For the plate, cut a piece of vinyl lace slightly larger than the plate. Spray the back of the lace with a light coat of stencil adhesive; press lace on the back side of the plate.

2 Sponge olive and seafoam green paints on back side of lace stencil until all openings are covered with paint as shown in Photo E. While paint is wet, carefully pull the lace off the plate. Let the paint dry.

3 To reveal the lace pattern, sponge the back of the plate with cream paint as shown in Photo F.

**4** For the vase, cut a piece of vinyl lace to cover the outside of the vase smoothly. Spray the back of the vinyl lace with a light coat of stencil adhesive; press lace around the vase.

**5** Sponge olive and seafoam green paints on back side of lace stencil until all openings are covered with paint. While paint is wet, carefully pull the vinyl lace off the vase. Let the paint dry.

**6** For both painted pieces, apply a clear gloss top coat if instructed by the paint manufacturer. Allow the glass pieces to dry 10 days before washing or as directed by the product label.

GIVE EACH PLACE SETTING A HINT OF VICTORIAN ELEGANCE WITH THE SAME LACY LOOK AS THE TABLETOP.

# WeLL-DresseD Lamp

## HERE'S HOW

1. In a well-ventilated work area, cover the work surface with newspapers. Remove the lampshade and set aside. Mask off areas to remain unpainted. Place the lamp on the newspapers; spray the lamp with one or two coats of chrome paint, allowing paint to dry between coats. Let dry.

2. Spray red glitter paint onto chrome paint. Let dry. Spray as many coats as needed to achieve the desired amount of glitter coverage. Let dry.

3. Spray on one or two coats of transparent red spray paint, allowing to dry between coats. Let dry.

4. Spray a portion of the lamp with copper paint if desired. Let dry.

5. Remove tape and paint remaining portion with black acrylic paint. Let dry.

**COMBINE FIVE PAINT COLORS, SOME SHEEN, AND GLITTER FOR SPARKLE TO CREATE A LAMP THAT WILL LIGHT UP ANY ROOM.**

## WHAT YOU'LL need

Newspapers; lamp

Masking tape

Spray paint in chrome and copper

Red lamé finish glitter paint, available at crafts stores

Red transparent spray paint, such as Dupli-Color Metalcast paint (available in automotive supply stores)

Black acrylic paint

Paintbrush

**before**

# COLORFUL
## surprises
### PAINTING
## unexpected pieces

Paint milkweed pods, cornhusks, and dried gourds? Put your brush to your suitcase or your kitchen utensils? You bet! This chapter helps your painting spirit soar with playful approaches that take only minutes but add loads of impact. And if you are looking for more involved projects, this chapter gives you those too. Try your hand at a woodburned table with a finish that looks like watercolor or a keepsake album personalized with words of endearment for someone special. You soon will be looking at all the items around your home as potential canvases for your painting passion!

143

# character
## cases

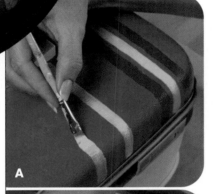

## WHAT YOU'LL need

Small suitcases

Masking tape; newspapers

Spray primer, such as KILZ

Acrylic enamels in orange, pink, green, and yellow

Medium flat and narrow artist's paintbrushes

Ruler; pencil with eraser

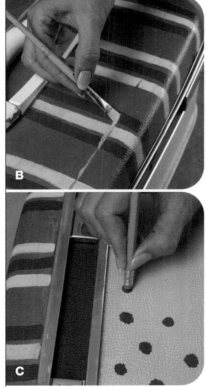

A

B

C

## here's HOW

**1** On a small suitcase, cover the hardware areas with masking tape. In a well-ventilated work area, cover work surface with newspapers. Spray the suitcase with primer. Let dry. Spray another coat. Let dry.

**2** For the small case, paint solid orange, pink, and green areas first. Let dry. Use a ruler to mark where lines are desired. For either suitcase, begin painting stripes, alternating colors such as pink and yellow using a flat paintbrush as shown in Photo A. Space the freehand lines as evenly as possible to keep the design uniform. Vary the width of lines using flat and narrow brushes as shown in Photo B.

**3** To make dots, dip the pencil eraser into paint and dot onto surface as shown in Photo C. Let dry.

GIVE A WELL-USED TOTE PERSONALITY
PLUS WITH BRIGHT PLAID AND PRETTY
POLKA DOTS.

# endearing album

A

B

## What you'll need

Newspapers; album; spray primer

Spray paint in metallic red or other desired color

Glossy gold paper

Paint sticks

Rubber painting brush

Spray adhesive

Clear spray sealer; metallic gold ribbon

## Here's how

**1** In a well-ventilated work area, cover the work surface with newspapers. To paint the album cover, take it apart if possible or lay it flat on newspapers. Spray album cover with one or two light coats of primer, allowing to dry between coats. Let dry after final coat.

**2** Spray the cover with one or two coats of spray paint. Let the paint dry between coats. Let final coat dry.

**3** Tear a piece of glossy gold paper slightly larger than the desired size. It is important to use a slick coated paper to facilitate writing.

**4** Use paint sticks to randomly color gold paper using heavy bold strokes as shown in Photo A. Fill in all areas of paper, blending one color over and into another. Note that red and yellow blend to make bright orange, red and purple blend to make burgundy, and blue and green make teal. Red and green or purple and yellow will result in brown. Opposite colors on the color wheel make subdued brown tones, such as blue and orange, purple and yellow, or red and green. Use colors next to each other to make brighter, purer color, such as red and orange, orange and yellow, yellow and green, green and blue, blue and purple, or purple and red.

**5** Use a rubber painting brush to write words of endearment or desired phrases as shown in Photo B. Frequently wipe off the paint from tip to keep the markings clean. Let the oil-based paints dry, which may take 24 hours.

**6** Tear the edges of the paper to the desired size. Use a gold paint pen to outline the torn edge. Let dry.

**7** Spray the back side of painted paper evenly with spray adhesive. Apply to surface.

**8** Spray a light, even coat of clear sealer over entire album. Let dry.

**9** Reassemble album. Tie a ribbon to binding of the book.

**WRITE SENTIMENTS ON A COLORFUL FIELD OF PAINT FOR AN ARTISTIC ALBUM COVER.**

# LAKESIDE TABLE

## WHAT YOU'LL NEED

Tracing paper

Pencil; scissors

Wood slab

Wood-burning tool

Pearlescent paints, such as Angelwings Enterprises Radiant Pearls, in green, pink, white, and blue

Soft wide paintbrush

Satin varnish

Driftwood; saw

½-inch plywood

Screws

Screwdriver

## HERE'S HOW

1 Trace the fish pattern, *page 151,* onto tracing paper; cut out and trace the outside shape in the center of the wood slab. To transfer the details, color the back side of fish pattern with a soft pencil, place it on the table, and trace the lines with a sharp pencil.

[continued on page 150]

USE A WOODBURNING TOOL TO DRAW A FISH
DESIGN, AND THEN THE WATERCOLOR-LOOK
PAINTING IS AS EASY AS PAINT BY NUMBER.

2 Draw over all lines using a woodburning tool as shown in Photo A.

3 To paint the fish, use a soft wide paintbrush. Practice first on an inconspicuous surface, using water to thin the pearlescent paints for easier blending. Referring to the photo on *page 149,* paint in green, pink, white, and blue areas, blending one color into another as shown in Photo B. Let the paint dry until color remains on surface when touched by your finger. This may take several days.

4 Coat the surface with a satin varnish. An aged varnish was used on this table for a brown tint. Let dry and coat again until the desired finish is achieved. Let dry.

5 Use a saw to cut three table legs from driftwood. Cut them one at a time and check the fit by placing the tabletop on top to make sure it sits level; adjust the legs until they support the top.

**6** Paint the legs using the same paints as for tabletop, blending one color into another. Let dry. Paint varnish on legs and let dry.

**7** Cut three small pieces of ½-inch plywood and screw each wood piece to the top end of a table leg. Attach table leg to the underside of the table by screwing the wood piece onto the tabletop as shown in Photo C. Make sure the screws are shorter than the thickness of the two layers of wood but long enough to hold the pieces together.

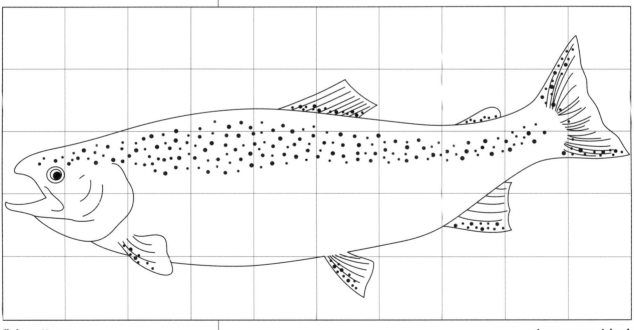

**fish pattern**

**1 square = 1 inch**

# Forever posies

**A**

**B**

KEEP THIS COLORFUL
DISPLAY BLOOMING ALL
YEAR LONG WITHOUT A
GREEN THUMB.

## WHAT YOU'LL need

Milkweed pods; hot-glue gun; glue sticks

Newspapers; small pinecones; sticks

Spray paints in orange, dark red, purple,
  teal, and yellow; scissors, if needed

Floral foam; small cardboard box

Sedum or any dried foliage; corn husks

## Here's HOW

1 Arrange milkweed pods into a flower
shape and hot-glue together.

2 In a well-ventilated work area, cover
work surface with newspapers. Spray
the inside of flower shape orange. Let dry.
Turn over and spray dark red. Let dry.

3 Spray the pinecones purple. Let dry.
Spray the sticks for stems using teal
and yellow. Let the paint dry.

4 To assemble flowers, hot-glue pinecone
in center and stem on the back.

5 Cut foam to fit in box. Place dried
sedum into foam piece. Spray with
dark red and highlight with purple or other
desired colors. Let dry.

6 Lay out pieces of cornhusks flat on
newspapers. Spray random spots of
teal, purple, and yellow, overlapping initial
areas to create green tones as shown in
Photos A and B. Let dry.

7 Hot-glue cornhusks on sides of box.
Trim off tops with scissors if needed.
Fold bottom edges under the box and glue
in place. Insert foam and sedum into box.
Insert flowers.

# KITCHEN TOOLS & SHAKERS

## HERE'S HOW

**1** Smooth any rough areas on wood using sandpaper; wipe away dust with a tack cloth. Avoid touching the areas to be painted.

**2** Cover the work surface with newspapers. Prime the wood sections to be painted; let dry. Paint the base colors and let dry.

**3** To make large dots, dip a pencil eraser into paint and dot onto the surface. For small dots, use a paintbrush handle. If layered dots are desired, let large dots dry before layering small dots.

**4** Continue creating designs on the wood pieces, painting spirals, stripes, wavy lines, or other simple motifs. Let the paint dry.

## WHAT YOU'LL NEED

Wood salt and pepper shakers or kitchen tools

Sandpaper; tack cloth

Newspapers

Primer, such as Kilz

Acrylic enamel paints, such as Liquitex Glossies

Paintbrush; pencil

HAVE FUN GRINDING PEPPER OR SCOOPING
ICE CREAM WITH PAINTED KITCHEN TIME
ITEMS THAT ARE FUNKY AND FUNCTIONAL.

# GLORIOUS GOURD HOUSES

## HERE'S HOW

**1** Clean and dry gourds with hot soapy water and a scrubber, removing mold and outer skin layer. Wipe dry.

**2** Use a 1-inch hole saw blade to cut a hole in the gourd. Drill a 3/16-inch hole below the larger hole for the perch. Cut 3/16-inch dowel for perch. Apply a small dab of wood glue and insert into hole.

**3** For the bird feeder, cut an oval shape in one side of the gourd.

**4** Mix powdered stain according to directions or use any liquid wood stain. Apply stain with a sponge applicator. Wipe off extra with a rag. Let dry.

**5** Use gold paint pens to draw repeated lines, dots, squiggles, outlines, or other desired designs. Detail the design using the narrow pen. To make the star, draw four triangles from the stem downward. Use the narrow pen to draw four more triangles in between the others.

**6** Spray the gourd with two light coats of sealer, allowing to dry between coats. Let dry. Hang with raffia.

## WHAT YOU'LL NEED

Gourds; hot soapy water; scrubber; rag

Drill with 1- and 3/16-inch hole saw blades

3/16-inch dowel; wood glue

Saw for making bird feeder

Powdered or liquid wood stains, such as Lockwood's Powdered Stains, in lemon yellow, mahogany, and bright blue

Sponge applicator

Wide and narrow metallic gold paint pens

Clear waterproof sealer; raffia

TREAT YOUR BACKYARD FRIENDS TO
EXTRA PRETTY PERCHES WITH THESE
GILDED GOURD BIRDHOUSES.

# index

# sources

## PAINTS

Angelwings–Radiant Pearls
3322 West Sussix Way
Fresno, CA 93722
800-400-3717
www.radiantpearls.com

Createx Colors
14 Airport Park Road
East Granby, CT 06026
800-243-2712

DecoArt
Highway 150 & 27
Stanford, KY 40484
800-367-3047
www.decoart.com

Design Master Color Tool, Inc.
P.O. Box 601
Boulder, CO 80306
303-443-5214
www.dmcolor.com

J.W. etc.
2205 First Street, Suite 103
Simi Valley, CA 93065
805-526-5066 (voice mail)
805-526-1297 (fax)
www.jwetc.com

Krylon Products Group
Cleveland, OH 44115
www.krylon.com
800-797-3332

McCloskey Special Effects
Division of Valspur Corp.
800-345-4530

Plaid Enterprises, Inc.
800-842-4197
678-291-8100
www.plaidonline.com

The Testor Corporation
440 Blackhawk Park Avenue
Rockford, IL 61104
800-962-6654

## SPRAY GLITTER

Floracraft Corp.
1 East Longfellow
Ludington, MI 49431
231-843-3401
www.floracraft.com

## project designers

Sue Banker 78–83
Carol Dahlstrom 58–59
Gayle Schadendorf 90–97,
   134–139
Alice Wetzel 16–23, 26–47,
   50–57, 60–71, 74–77,
   84–85, 98–107, 110–133,
   140–141, 144–157
Sharon Widdop 24–25,
   86–89

## PHOTO STYLING

Carol Dahlstrom

## PHOTO STYLING assistant

Donna Chesnut